"Jane Baxter shows a path out of depression using regular exercise . . . and empowers people to take more control of their recovery as they become healthier and happier."

— Robert L. DuPont, MD
Author of *The Anxiety Cure* and *The Anxiety Cure For Kids*

"The authoritative resource on exercise and its application to treating and preventing depressive symptoms and episodes . . . Dr. Baxter's book is an essential part of contemporary management of depression."

— Roger S. McIntyre, MD, FRCPC
Associate Professor of Psychiatry and Pharmacolgy,
University of Toronto;
Head, Mood Disorders Psychopharmacology Unit

:, well written . . . it's a perfect 'take.'"

— Joey Pantoliano
Grammy Award-Winning Actor,
President & Founder, *No Kidding, Me Too!*
www.nkm2.org

"Jane Baxter combines her expertise as a therapist as well as her knowledge of regular exercise to show how persons suffering from depression may find a new approach to developing confidence and being able to change. Baxter paints an upward path to overcoming negative feelings and moving beyond being a victim of the disease. I strongly recommend this book. "

— Dale Masi, PhD
Author of *Shrink to Fit* and
Productivity Lost: Alcohol and Drugs in the Workplace

Manage Your Depression through Exercise

Manage Your Depression through Exercise

The Motivation You
Need to Start
and Maintain an
Exercise Program

JANE BAXTER

SUNRISE
River Press

39966 Grand Avenue
North Branch, MN 55056
Phone: 651-277-1400 or 800-895-4585
Fax: 651-277-1203
www.sunriseriverpress.com

Edit by Karen Chernyaev
Layout by Monica Seiberlich
All photos by Charles Martin

ISBN 978-1-934716-24-3
Item No. SRP624

Library of Congress Cataloging-in-Publication Data

Baxter, Jane.
  Manage your depression through exercise : a five-week plan to a happier, healthier you by / Jane Baxter.
    p. cm.
  Includes index.
  ISBN 978-1-934716-24-3
1. Depression, Mental--Exercise therapy--Popular works. 2. Self-care, Health--Popular works. I. Title.
  RC537.B347 2011
  616.85'27062--dc22

                         2011011856

Printed in USA
10 9 8 7 6 5 4 3 2 1

Dedication

To my most cherished children, Natalie, Michelle, and Cal

Contents

Illustrations

Preface

"If you treat an individual as he is, he will stay as he is,
but if you treat him as if he were what he ought to be and could be,
he will become what he ought to be and could be."
— Johann Wolfgang von Goethe

I wish I could meet you in person. There is so much that happens in a person-to-person session, and, with that in mind, I have written this book as if you were sitting with me. Picking up this book is an act of courage—and you have much to gain by it. As you go through the pages you'll capture important feelings and insights and will no longer feel like a victim of depression. Rather, you will experience being a creator of your new life. When working together, this book and you become very powerful.

Motivation is in many ways an interpersonal process—the product of an interaction between people. For that reason, I wish I knew you personally. You will get a sense of me, as my personality will undoubtedly come through my writing. Although I will most likely not get to know you, I have sat with many, many women and men in your situation. I have heard heart-breaking stories and have been able to work with individuals as they take control of their stories and work toward some pretty terrific midlife chapters. As a practicing psychotherapist, I have had the honor of bearing witness to fabulous transformations. And so I have written this book with a general sense of what you may be experiencing. I hope this comes through in our interaction.

Science is starting to prove what readers have known all along: The written word can help you repair and revitalize your body as well as your mind. Whether the problem is physical discomfort, emotional conflict or suffering, or relational problems in the family, at work, or in the community, reading specific texts in response to particular situations or conditions can change and improve how you feel and behave. Success lies in the combination of the reading process itself and the content. The words in this book will stimulate the creation of mental images that further draw you into the text; you will act out the words on the page in your mind. You then become the creator of your own inner word document, which then translates into *your* authentic, subjective text.

Studies that scan the brains of readers who are mesmerized in their books show that some of the regions active during reading are the same as those brain regions used when people perform or observe real-life activities. Our brains mirror what happens in the story as if the same thing were happening to us "live." In our imagination we become part of the action. Other studies show that reading contributes to cognitive reserve, the brain's ability to protect itself and to adapt to physical damage. Guided self-help interventions with patients who are depressed, anxious, or phobic have had comparable effects to traditional face-to-face psychotherapy sessions, and the blend of these forms of therapy will be occurring more and more in the future.

You won't just be sitting back and reading, however. While this book is about lifting you out of your depression through exercise, it also addresses how to get motivated to do so. Motivation is its own state, one that needs to be fertilized and nurtured throughout life. Loneliness, anger, and low self-esteem are psychic thieves that rob you of motivation and leave you stuck in your depression. I will be talking about these dynamics throughout the book, and I hope to shepherd you through the jungles that these issues represent. In following along with me, you'll find yourself honing your own expertise and perspective on yourself and your life and evoking the resources and motivation for change that are already within you.

How important would you say it is for you to exercise to feel better? On a scale of 0-10, where 0 is not at all important and 10 is extremely important, where would you say you are? And, if you decided to exercise consistently, how confident are you that you'd follow through? On the same scale of 0-10, where 0 is not at all confident and 10 is extremely confident, where would you say you are?

That simple exercise is to help you see that there is a difference between the importance of change and your confidence about change. And that these are actually interrelated. If you don't feel that change is important, then confidence isn't that important either. If you do feel it is important, but you have low confidence, then that affects your perceived ability. For the most part, depression doesn't yield high confidence. So we will continue to work on that throughout the book, getting you to the place where change and confidence meet.

This book includes many exercises that tap your self-perceptions, goals, and values, so by the end you will literally have written this book with me. And I hope you will e-mail me your exercises, so that I *can* get to know you and bear witness to your courage.

Introduction

In recent years, research has proven what we intuitively know to be true: Exercise helps to heal depression. Most people suffering from depression know this as well, just as overweight people know what foods they should eat in order to lose weight. Yet knowing and doing are two different dynamics. In this book, you're going to learn a lot of information about how exercise affects depression. You may already be familiar with some of it, but a large percentage of it may be new to you, including the effect of exercise on brain chemistry and life experiences. Even if you are well-versed in all the latest research on exercise and depression, this book is meant to provide the missing link between knowing and doing, which for most people is motivation and accountability.

In this book, I supply two critical tools to help lift you out of your depression: positive thinking and exercise. For many people, these tools prove to be healing. After applying them over the course of five weeks, most people feel their depression lift to varying degrees. I won't be able to assess how you're doing, so it's important that you keep your doctor(s) informed of your progress so that you can collaborate on the important decision of whether to stay on or adjust any medication(s) you may be taking.

Although exercise has the capacity to change lives, it's not a panacea. Each of us has our own unique biochemistry and life history, which means every one of us requires our own blend of treatment. In some cases, a consistent exercise regimen may be the ticket to health. In other cases, exercise needs to complement a more rigorous medical intervention. Regardless of whether you've got a mild case of the blues or treatment-resistant clinical depression, exercise helps to alleviate symptoms. If you currently exercise routinely and still suffer from depressive symptoms, you may find some additional information here that will help you improve your current regimen. Whatever your situation, bear in mind that exercise is not necessarily a substitute for medication or therapy.

For nearly a decade, I have worked with hundreds of depressed patients in what I call PsychFit, a program that combines the healing benefits of psychotherapy and exercise, and they all fear the same thing upon starting. It goes something like this: "If I get off to a good start, I am afraid I can't keep it going, and then when I stop and can't get restarted, I feel like a failure, worse than when I began."

One of your goals in this program is to keep your eye on today. Today, or right now to be exact, is the only time when things can start to pull together, stay the same, or continue spiraling downward. Right now you're doing something positive for yourself. If you start thinking about how you're sure to mess it up in the future, you've left the moment. So come on back to now, because if you reach that point at which you imagine you will fail, it becomes "right now" again. It's kind of beautiful how that works.

1

Week One — On Your Mark, Get Set, Read!

Depression resides in the brain, which is the most complex object in the universe, consisting of 100 billion neurons and roughly ten times as many other cells that have supportive roles. At the end of each neuron are synapses. Exercise, we now know, helps these synapses to function better; strong and well-functioning connections between synapses allow for the most learning and development. Throughout this book, you will learn a combination of specific physical and mental exercises that will create a powerful system by which your depression can heal, your mind can brighten, and your body can thrive.

You and I are going to be spending a lot of time together, so let's get started by talking about Day One of your program. That's all, just Day One, because, despite what your depression might be telling you, "right now" is the only time you really have to do anything about your situation.

First, I'm going to cover what it takes to build a good foundation for an exercise program. A good foundation includes having the right frame of mind. It also involves adjusting some beliefs—beliefs your depression would rather hold onto. Once you have a good foundation, you'll be able to build a great program for yourself.

Building a Foundation

Building a strong foundation requires learning to stay focused in the moment and being able to counter the destructive minivoice within. It also requires understanding some basic beliefs and attitudes.

Depression has its own pessimistic and distracting minivoice—a voice that has nothing to do with "right now." This small but powerful voice keeps you focused on what you can't do in the future and takes you away from what you really do have, which is the present moment.

The first thing you need to do is to tell that voice to stop distracting you. "Okay Jane," you might be thinking, "I got the voice to quiet down, but I still have this feeling that's hard to describe—a feeling of dread tinged with a little anxiety." I know that feeling. It will be lingering for the next week or so, and it is important to tolerate it and know that it will go away as you continue to practice staying in the moment, being in the "right now."

How do I know it will go away? Until now, your depression has been running the show, and it wants to stay in charge. But as you practice staying in the moment you learn to trust that you can stay focused. That's right. All you have to do is simply stay focused right now. You will build on this with each "now" moment, day after day. And when you get to that three-week period, that point where you think you might start to slip, guess what? It's "right now" again.

You will also build confidence as you continue to do your daily practice, which involves simple physical exercises and some mental redirection. The biggest redirection you will be giving the minivoice of your depression is to chill out and stop living in the wreckage of the future. Your fear will dissipate as you do all you can right now to be healthy by doing the exercises and practicing a positive attitude, even if you don't necessarily feel positive.

I want to give you a few strong arguments for countering your depression's minivoice, specifically, optimism, positive thinking, and meditation. By absorbing these countering arguments, you develop your own positive, disputing response that you will remember and pull out like a handy quick-fix tool from your back pocket. Think of it as planting the seeds of positive thinking so that the weeds of depression get crowded out and cannot grow. Exercise will be like the sun and water and fertilizer, helping the positive thoughts to grow and strengthening their support-ive neurological networks (more about exercise and brain chemistry in Chapter 6).

This chapter covers several important concepts that will help you to build a strong foundation. Once you understand them, you'll begin the process of shifting your brain out of its depression gear. Foundation-building attitudes and beliefs include conviction, a "bring it" attitude, optimism, exiting the comparing-yourself-to-others torture chamber, and the importance of claiming your life. Finally, you will begin the exercises for the first week and learn how to track your progress.

Before I continue, I would like you to fill out Chart 1.1 (see page 6) so that we have a baseline of where your feelings are right now. You will be able to see the positive changes over the next several weeks as you fill out this form again at weeks three and five.

Conviction

The word "conviction" applies to a lasting, habituated state of mind car-ried over into action. Conviction is the end product, not the starting point, of your choices. But it is the end product of *each* choice, not of the entire process. The fact that you bought this book is a choice. It was the start of deciding to "go for it." You then took action by opening and reading the first page. You believe you have the ability to change; otherwise, you would not have "gone for it." As you continue to make positive choices, your conviction grows. As you continue to believe in yourself, page-by-page, step-by-step, you will come to realize that you really can build a happy, meaningful life. You will understand more deeply that this requires not only a choice but also acting on that choice. Conviction grows when you do what you say you're going to do.

Depression creates transient states of mind, so even when you are sin-cere in your belief that you want to pull out of it, you may not have an enduring conviction. Depression creates distortions, tries to keep you in its old patterns of thoughts and actions (or inactions as the case may be), and deflates your belief. Belief without action is just a wish; belief with action is called conviction.

Chart 1.1	**Your Feelings**			
During the past week...	**Rarely or none of the time (<1 day)**	**Some (a little of the time) (1–2 days)**	**At least half the time (3–4 days)**	**Just about all the time (5–7 days)**
1. I was bothered by things that usually don't bother me.	0	1	2	3
2. I did not feel like eating; my appetite was poor.	0	1	2	3
3. I could not shake off the blues, even with others' help.	0	1	2	3
4. I felt that I was just as good as other people.	3	2	1	3
5. I had trouble keeping my mind on what I was doing.	0	1	2	0
6. I felt depressed.	0	1	2	3
7. I felt that everything I did was an effort.	0	1	2	3
8. I felt hopeful about the future.	3	2	1	0
9. I thought my life had been a failure.	0	1	2	3
10. I felt fearful.	0	1	2	3
11. My sleep was restless.	0	1	2	3
12. I was happy.	3	2	1	0
13. I talked less than usual.	0	1	2	3
14. I felt lonely.	0	1	2	3
15. People were unfriendly.	0	1	2	3
16. I enjoyed life.	3	2	1	0
17. I had crying spells.	0	1	2	3
18. I felt sad.	0	1	2	3
19. I felt that people disliked me.	0	1	2	3
20. I could not "get going."	0	1	2	3

Scoring: Your score is the sum of all twenty circled numbers. You will be comparing your score from week one to week three to week five. A decreasing score shows that your depression is getting better.

The Ability to Choose

Some writers have viewed the capacity to choose as being the defining quality of humankind. Philosopher Jean-Paul Sartre took the position that man "is" his choices. It is important that you know that there is very little to prevent you from choosing to learn new thinking processes. When you do learn new thinking and behaving patterns, you can choose to make the corrective thinking a habitual pattern in your daily life. You then base your choices on reason, not on what your depressed feelings are telling you. These steps are critical—and doable. Without them, you will most likely not see results. Right now your depression most likely makes most decisions for you. I will guide you toward increasing *your* capacity to make choices.

The Ability to Act

Action is predicated on a rational view of certain options. We make so many of our choices based on feelings; you know, the old "I don't feel like it" voice. The rational voice, however, says, "I don't feel like it, but I know that I can push through it for the next twenty minutes and nothing bad will happen. In fact, I know I will feel better because I checked something off that blasted list that has been driving me crazy for weeks." The choice to get better lies within you—it's your life. I will show you the way by teaching and correcting.

I want you to comprehend the monumental importance of your choice regarding exercise. There are only two options here. One option is to stay the same, to continue living with cycles of depression and their accompanying lack of zest for life. The second option is change. At first, this change only requires that you set up daily appointments with yourself to work this program with me every day until we are finished and that you trust the moment, now.

No Excuses, Please!

For some time now, you have been enduring the consequences of your depression-soaked choices, so please embrace the following "tough love" statement: *Excuses are not welcome.* You are personally responsible for what course you take, you are not a victim of the thoughts that pass through your mind, and the burden of the decision to try to get better rests on you. The fact that certain habits are longstanding is meaningless. I accept no excuses.

Depression operates on excuses. Eliminating the "I can't do it" or "I don't care, this is just who I am" attitude is, in many cases, easier than you may think. You've never read this book before, have you? You've never tried to heal exactly this way before, right? So, tell that doubting mini-voice to zip it. You are in charge, not "it." Tell it over and over again. One day it will stop.

Committing to an exercise program of recovery is a matter of making a responsible choice. In the beginning, you will be choosing to take the program on faith, even when you don't feel like it is working. You will also need to choose to do what you said you would do, regardless of whether you are interested, like it, or are given a guarantee of success. On some days, this may require altering a victim or "I can't" stance. To be in a position to make responsible choices, you must choose to see yourself as you truly are, and this may mean adopting a different view of yourself—an "I can" view. In adopting this new and more accurate view of yourself, you may find it helpful to ask trusted family members and friends to help you gain perspective on what is real and what is depression chatter.

Later in this chapter, you'll do an exercise that will help you to see your current thinking process and to learn how to replace the depressive thoughts. As you learn about recognizing the negative spin depression puts on everything and then dispute or counter the spin, you essentially learn a new method of processing through the dialogue that goes on in your head. The drive to work this hard at it comes from the ultimate existential question: What kind of life do you want? Remember, the two options are to remain as you are and never fulfill your potential (and perhaps die never knowing it), or to take the leap of faith to work and implement what is being asked of you. If not now, when?

I will be repeatedly making an issue of this ultimate choice and asking you to focus on it throughout the book. Learning new thought processes is one choice in the process of change, and this choice gains effectiveness only though implementation. Implementation is an option to be chosen over and over again.

Ability Is Not the Issue

Let's talk about the idea of saying, "I can't." When truly challenged, you know that ability is not the issue. So choose not to go there. Refusing to accept your potential is incompatible with making and implementing responsible choices. It is important to know that depression-generated thoughts won't cease immediately. It happens over time, and the fact that these thoughts continue is not evidence that you are unable to change. Expect that these thoughts will recur for a while but that if you acquire and implement the recognition-dispute method (see Chapter 6), you will preempt the occurrence of such thoughts, which is what we're aiming for. With practice, you will begin to automatically preempt and squelch the thoughts coming from your depression.

Eliminate all excuses in favor of a mental set of "I can!" and then a mental set of "I get to!" (as opposed to "I have to"). The correction for this thinking error is the attitude of doing the difficult now. It's more than the elimination of excuses. It is *doing*—doing the program.

Overcoming depression happens at first in moments—moments you most likely have experienced. All you need to do is add to the moments. I am confident that you can join the scores of others who have one day at a time moved into a healthier, happier way of living.

"Bring It" Attitude

Do you have the conviction needed to implement this program? If you don't think you do, that's okay. We will work on it one step at a time. In the meantime, you may need to promise yourself that you'll not just follow along but "bring it," one day at a time. If you stay with me, the conviction will come.

If you do have the conviction, will you demonstrate it by having a "bring it" attitude each week? You've seen scenes in a TV show or movie where one person has a score to settle with another and they give that person the "bring it" look. Half-hearted efforts or "giving it a try" don't typically work for long. "Bringing it" is one choice—a choice you will live into. The outcome of this choice and all your hard work, even though you might not like it at the time, is valuable beyond words. It's both fun and not fun, but it gives you the self-respect and peace of mind to become a whole person again by doing right by yourself and by the people who love and care about you. Whether you know it or not, doing something good for yourself has a positive ripple effect—your actions help all those who care about you, as your depression makes their lives less than full. The truth is they have been struggling with you by having to work on their issues around control, helplessness, and patience.

Letting Go

If you want to change out of convenience rather than conviction, or if you want to change only if it's easy or you can be guaranteed a certain result in a certain period of time, it's time to let go of that mindset. Your goal is not going to be to lose fifteen pounds or drop two sizes, although those kinds of results are entirely possible. The goal is to feel better, one day at a time, and to let your body move into its natural physical and mental state. The rest will follow. Right now I need you to be sincere about wanting to start your exercise program for the right reasons.

If you have reservations, your depression is doing its thing. I expect that you will have wavering desire. When you feel doubt, sit with it and let it pass. Like waves of the ocean crashing on the shore and falling back to the sea, let your ambivalence recede and make room for a steady and growing stream of determination and action.

Endurance

Endurance means doing what has to be done whether you feel like it or not. You alone are responsible for developing your endurance. It cannot be taught by anybody else or given to you by anyone else. Throughout the first several weeks of this program, consider your feelings to be subordinate to reason. A big part of this program is telling the truth to yourself first and foremost—that you need to get better and that you will not be receiving any medals for your efforts. You will surmount any obstacle rather than quit or fall back to the depression. I call this kind of endurance "will" (meaning the "will" to exercise—not willpower over your depression).

Some people fail to implement a responsible choice, even though they are sincere, and they fail because they do not want to endure the transitional discomfort that comes with new choices and behaviors. But the discomfort is only transitional. Early on, your healthy choices (each of which leads to other healthy choices) may leave you feeling as if you're in a kind of a no man's land—a place barren of the activities familiar to you and your depression. If you look at Chart 1.1, which you just filled out, you will know what activities I am talking about. But feelings of unfamiliarity, or the sense that something is "off," aren't bad. In fact, it means you're making progress. This "off" feeling is just your brain's way of holding onto what's been safe and secure (even if not happy) for you, and it's only temporary. All will start to feel better as you and your brain ease into your new "normal."

Choice and will are complementary. Choice cannot be implemented without endurance or will. The more successful the implementation, the stronger you affirm each choice you make.

As you get more distance from your depression, intermittently relive the harm that it has done. Facing up to this past again and again is necessary to discard the old patterns. You cannot realistically evaluate your progress in the program without contrasting present thinking and

The 24-Hour Record

Are you ready for your first task? Grab a notebook and pen (a small notebook is ideal as you can carry it with you). The assignment is to pretend that a camcorder is recording your thoughts and behaviors over a twenty-four-hour period (excluding sleep time). Write down any depressed thoughts, inner dialogue, and behaviors that the camcorder is recording. You won't be able to collect all your thoughts; focus on the thoughts and behaviors that uphold your depression. You will need to tune into the raw data of your thinking, reporting in detail what your depression is saying to you and how you respond. You pretty much know the times of day that pose a problem for you, and when you pinpoint these times and start to understand them better, you will allow your instincts (versus your depression) to give you a more accurate picture of the truth.

The 24-Hour Record exercise forces you to scrutinize your current thinking and the distorted convictions your depressive thoughts may have committed you to. (Yes, it is possible to have conviction for destructive behaviors.) You may report your thoughts chronologically (attaching them to events or conversations) or thematically (grouping them under headings such as TV-watching, Food, Triggers, Relationships with friends, family, and work).

Another goal of this exercise is for you to see in black and white that feelings are not facts but merely pretend to reveal facts, sometimes deceiving you or leading you in the wrong direction.

Thoughts alone possess the quality of fact or fiction. Let's take the following scenario: you are riding the metro and your stop comes and goes, you realize this as the doors close and the next stop is announced. You say to yourself, "I feel like such an idiot." What you're describing is a neurotically generated feeling, but the truth is that you are most likely tired, distracted and maybe have low blood sugar. An idiot is a person of subnormal intelligence. Your depression can be so hard on you, can't it?"

People feel worse if they are unhappy and have no idea why. If you think about your feelings and actions when you are unhappy, you will take comfort in knowing the cause and how it can be changed. In dealing with your emotions and life satisfaction, you need to notice patterns. As many of my patients have said, "The more I write, the more progress I make." They have all found that their notes are valuable in unearthing destructive thought patterns, and so will you.

Those who let themselves exist in the midst of random events not only don't understand what is happening to them, they also can't do anything to change their world. Those who are least likely to overcome a temporary sense of dissatisfaction with life are those who cannot identify the sources of their feelings.

The self-analysis that you are required to develop (the healthy criticism of your depression's distorted point of view) has to occur with ensuing corrections. Otherwise, it is just a confession and a confession alone does not ensure change.

Use this exercise to learn how to recognize depressed thinking and to question it at all times. Concentrate on your choices and the risks you take if you return to beliefs and choices your depression manufactures. You cannot be committed to the responsibility of getting healthy while maintaining that you are a victim and offering excuses.

action with what has been characteristic of your earlier patterns and how you succumbed or became resigned to your illness while depressed.

You have had the vague idea for some time that you would need to take on your depression, no-holds-barred. And now that day is here.

Optimism

Winston Churchill once said a pessimist sees difficulty in every opportunity, and an optimist sees opportunity in every difficulty. Oscar Wilde said that the basis of optimism is sheer terror. George F. Will said that the nice part about being a pessimist is that you are constantly being either proven right or pleasantly surprised. Optimism is what pessimism is not, so let's look at pessimism first.

Pessimism is now recognized as a strong risk factor for depression, mainly because it has the effect of bringing personal, creative, and professional endeavors to a halt and becomes a self-fulfilling prophecy. A pessimist doesn't think something will work and either gives up or doesn't even begin.

Pessimism can be a curse if it makes you give up your goals and dreams. But unfounded optimism, the belief that everything will turn out fine without the necessary effort, has the same effect. Optimism is a wonderful state of mind, but having a slightly cautious understanding of reality can be helpful as well.

Becoming more optimistic requires you to understand how your thoughts, feelings, and behavior are interrelated and can be reworked to increase optimism. The exercise in "The 24-Hour Record" sidebar on page 11 is a great tool for getting yourself to see how the three affect one another.

Fake It Till You Make It

Anyone can learn optimism by, well, just doing it. I tell patients that it's usually much easier to change behavior than feelings or thoughts. So, act like an optimist until you start feeling like one: Fake it till you make it. Your thoughts and feelings become more optimistic as you behave more optimistically. Again, this kind of learned optimism bears no resemblance whatsoever to the belief that merely wishing something is so will make it so. Your beliefs do influence what happens to you, and true optimism is just as much about action as it is about attitude. It's not enough to think positively, you also have to work to make positive things happen; and that most likely means working through a thick layer of negativity.

In the ensuing weeks, you will get better and better at becoming aware of how a pessimistic sequence of thoughts, feelings, and behaviors may try to undermine your fitness goals. And, subsequently, you will more easily be able to distance or distract yourself from those negative thoughts. Remember also that pessimistic beliefs are not facts.

Let's use going to the gym as an example. You may think you look terrible, but who is looking at you? Most people in the gym are too preoccupied with their own insecurities and routine to pay much attention to you. And if they do notice you, it may be with a good deal of respect and admiration for your efforts. You can also learn to replace a negative thought, such as "Ugh, I am such a load. Look at all these skinny and gorgeous people," with a more grounded thought: "First of all, I am way more than my looks; second, I am blowing this out of proportion—exercise is necessary for my good health as well as for looking fit." The outcome may be that you return to the gym, this time with your goals in mind.

Whenever you exercise, whether it involves an intense workout or just a regular long walk, you will feel healthier and better about yourself, and you will enjoy life more. A patient of mine used to say, "Whenever the thought occurs to me that maybe I should exercise, I lie down until the thought passes." He said this a lot, and, not surprisingly, his philosophy led him directly to a lack of energy and, soon, to health problems including a deeper depression. After I impressed on him the necessity of changing his lifestyle, he gave it a try. Gradually, he found he actually enjoyed exercising. It was a chance to spend some time, every day, without any worries or concerns, doing something positive. And instead of making him tired, exercise increased his energy. What's his mindset now? "I enjoy exercise so much I can hardly put it into words." Exercise will increase your self-confidence, which in turn will strengthen both your optimism and conviction.

Let Your Goals Evolve

Some individuals have come into my office upset because they cannot attain their goals, and they are consumed with disappointment. This is an understandable reaction, especially if the goals were based on unfounded optimism. Optimistic people who are grounded in reality know how to let their goals evolve with their life circumstances. They may experience great disappointment, but they know how to move forward.

Throughout the next few weeks, you will be updating your goals as you consider your changing priorities and resources. Goals are important, but they will do you a great disservice if they are not grounded and flexible. Following is a good example, as well as a fairly typical story.

Janice became engaged at the age of twenty-eight, and her wedding date was set for two years later. She was determined to lose twenty pounds in that two-year period. She had just been promoted at work to a managerial level, leading a team of fifty people. To get in shape for her wedding, she decided to try a liquid diet for three weeks while working out at the gym five days a week. She was not able to keep up with that, so she decided to join Weight Watchers. She did well the first month with her eating, but could not make it to the gym, and because her work was so stressful, she was unable to work out at home. She spent her weekends planning the wedding: trying on dresses, meeting with caterers, meeting with floral designers, and looking for just the right setting for the reception. Month after month went by and her eating habits began to slip. She was unable to get to the gym more than two times a week, and she was growing impatient with her fiancé, whom she felt was not as helpful as she needed him to be. She started to become depressed and overwhelmed. After the first year of being engaged, she needed to travel for work, which took her away from the wedding planning, her gym, and her Weight Watchers meetings. In desperation, she started doing Weight Watchers too rigidly and was therefore feeling deprived. She developed even worse habits eating out while traveling and became more and more frustrated.

Janice was both missing her fiancé and also becoming more frustrated with him. They were having more arguments and disagreements about the wedding, and she was feeling concerned about their relationship. She started binge eating, which reversed the progress she had made on the Weight Watchers plan. She panicked as she started putting on weight and became more depressed.

Had Janice only realized from the start that working out two to three days a week and eating well-balanced meals, while cutting out the junk food, would have sufficed, she would have been far less stressed during this period. Just these small changes would have helped her lose the weight and stay centered. And, she would have had a better, more satisfying relationship with her fiancé.

By the time she came in to see me, Janice felt completely demoralized. I said to her, "Hey, cheer up, nothing is that awful. You are engaged to a great guy, you have a great job, and we can figure this out day by day. It is important to realize that your goals could not have worked out given what was going on in your life over the past eighteen months. So let's get more realistic and get you into a good eating plan where you are not feeling deprived and into a fun exercise routine that will help you with your stress, as well as create a calorie deficit, so that you can lose some weight. Keep in mind that people don't see you for that ten- or twenty- pound difference that you see yourself. They see you with your smile, your great life, your big personality, and your generous and caring heart."

She followed my guidance and, sure enough, became very relieved that things felt more in control, which helped her become less depressed. Her change in behavior and attitude reversed her dark mood and helped her become more cheerful and optimistic. Janice was back to her old self, looking forward to her wedding. She did take off some weight, felt great in her dress, and realized that she need not be so self-absorbed.

If your goals are incongruent with your abilities, the goals will increase the likelihood of your being dissatisfied. If you have goals that are not too overwhelming, that you can achieve every day, you will be quite pleased with your progress.

Be Your Own Biggest Fan

When you're depressed, it's easy to take a situation you are uncertain about and come to a negative conclusion. For example, if you aren't sure why another person is being nice to you, you might assume that the person has a hidden agenda. Any situation can be viewed as an act of selfishness, if that's how you want to view it. Taking this perspective makes you cold, critical, and cynical. And there's no way out of it, because the person you are viewing negatively cannot do anything to improve your impression of him. The power is in your hands. You need to consider that your perspective on what motivates people can either be a source of comfort to you or a source of concern.

Optimistic people and depressed people explain their worlds differently. When an unhappy person must interpret the world, he most often sees the negative in any event. When a happy person must interpret the world, she more than likely sees the positive.

We assume that happy and unhappy people are born that way. But both kinds of people do things that create and reinforce their moods. Happy people let themselves be happy. Depressed people continue doing things that upset them and keep them stuck. For example: What is the first sign of a healthy business? A healthy business plan. A healthy business plan shows the definition and the purpose of the business; and, it lays out a strategy to accomplish that purpose. Happy people rely on an internal, and often unconscious, business plan. This same approach can be used in your personal life. I will be helping you to define what you want, using a strategy that combines exercise and mental corrections.

Happy, optimistic people do not experience win after win while depressed people experience failure after failure. Instead, the research shows that optimistic and depressed people tend to have very similar life experiences. The difference is that the average depressed person spends more than twice as much time thinking about unpleasant things and events in their lives, while happy or optimistic people tend to seek and rely on information and people that brighten their personal outlook and lifestyle.

Bad things happen, but usually we do not feel the effects forever. It's really true that time heals wounds. Your disappointments are important and serious, but there is a chance that your depression will pass for good, and your life will take you in new directions. If it doesn't pass, you will have an incredible cadre of tools to use as you recognize its cycles; you will be able to shorten the downward spiral and not live in the fear that you are powerless over it.

Give yourself some time. Studies of thousands of Americans show that happy people are not immune to negative events. Instead, happy people are characterized by the ability to think about other things in the aftermath of negative events. Be your own fan. We all need self-reinforcement, a belief in ourselves that is strong and unwavering.

If you had a challenge ahead of you—such as trying to climb a mountain or finishing a big project at work—what kind of people would you want to be surrounded by? Pessimistic people who reminded you why you were likely to fail? Or optimistic people who rallied around you to support you because they knew you would succeed?

Think of the people you like to be around. Think of the people who are a joy to be around. What do they have in common? Are any of them pessimistic—continually expecting the worst to happen? Living a satisfied life is one of the defining challenges of your life, and it is a challenge best met with optimism.

Exiting the Comparison Torture Chamber

One of the biggest disservices you can do to yourself is to compare yourself to others. It is just a one-way ticket into a self-induced torture chamber, especially when you are depressed. Many of our feelings of satisfaction or dissatisfaction have their roots in how we compare ourselves to others. When we compare ourselves to those who have more, look better, or do more, we feel bad. When we compare ourselves to those who have less, we tend to feel grateful. Even though the truth is we have exactly the same life either way, our feelings about our life can vary tremendously based on whom we compare ourselves with.

People who are satisfied appreciate what they have in life and don't worry about how it compares to what others have. Valuing what you have over what you do not have or cannot have leads to greater happiness. Why remind yourself of the things in life you don't have when you could remind yourself of what you do have? Studies show that people who have the most are just as likely to be happy and satisfied as those who have the least. People who like what they have, however, are twice as likely to be happy as those who have the most. The moral of the story? Be grateful for who you are and what you have. Following is a case in point:

> A large group of students was given a word puzzle to solve. Researchers compared the satisfaction of students who finished the puzzle quickly and those who finished more slowly. Students who finished the puzzle quickly and compared themselves with the very fastest students came away feeling dissatisfied with themselves. Students who finished the puzzle more slowly but compared themselves with the slowest students came away feeling quite satisfied with themselves and tended to ignore the presence of the quick-finishing students.

A Work in Progress

You are, just like everyone else, an almost inconceivably complicated mix of abilities and limitations. Instead of dwelling on something you think is wrong and resolving to improve it, take a different approach. Resolve to accept yourself right now as a work in progress. Acknowledge that, faults and all, you are a complete person and a very good person at that. Accepting yourself does not mean that you ignore your faults and never try to improve. What it does mean is that believing in your own words first, last, and always is of utmost importance and, in fact, a priority.

Set Meaningful Goals

Focus on what matters to you. There is no point in competing in a game that you don't really care to win. Don't allow your life and expectations to become anything but deeply personal reflections of what matters the most to you. Many of us are constantly in competitions where we don't really want the prize. What is your goal? Were you born to get promoted before one of your co-workers? Were you born to get a better car than your neighbor? Let your life goals guide you, not meaningless competitions that distract you from what is important to your heart and soul. Meaningful goals are crucial to your orientation to the world and to life satisfaction.

Realize that complete satisfaction does not exist. Set your sights on being generally satisfied and generally happy, not on expecting every aspect of life to be perfect. Complete satisfaction does not exist because everything can be improved upon. Those who accept this can appreciate what they have. Those who do not accept this can never appreciate what they have even as their circumstances improve. They see what others are doing and then judge themselves as "less than."

Strive to improve. Don't try to be perfect. Those who believe they will fail to achieve their goals are unhappy, but so are those who believe they will meet each goal just the way they imagined it. Those who are happiest believe they will meet some of their goals and will receive satisfaction from multiple aspects of their life.

You do not have to succeed in everything you do to feel happy. But you do have to believe you are maintaining some measure of control over your life. In fact, those who feel that they are responsible for their position and decisions express much more life satisfaction than those who do not.

People are happiest when they allow their individual personality to come out, not when they conform to popular images. For example, some men believe they must act fast and some women believe they must act soft, and they then box themselves into a set of expectations that has nothing to do with who they really are. Another example is that people with many friends sometimes yearn for a closer family, and people with a close family sometimes yearn for more friends. The key to continued satisfaction with life is not in replicating what someone else has. Instead, build a support system that you draw from and that gives to you, regardless of whether it is made up of primarily friends or family.

Perhaps a classmate at your high school reunion is richer, prettier, and smarter than everybody else. Does it matter? Your life is shaped more by your everyday relationships than by the life of acquaintances you see only rarely. Sometimes we look at what other people have, and we want that instead of thinking about what really and truly motivates us, what we really and truly want and need. Don't take someone else's accomplishment as evidence that you are doing anything wrong. Satisfaction with life is typically found to be related to experiences with family and friends, those with regular participation in life, and is typically unrelated to those with whom contact is brief or irregular. The best internal dialogue when you see that classmate is, "So what?" And, if you can swing it, "I'm happy for her."

Researchers have identified the core factors of a happy life as number of friends, closeness of friends, closeness of family, and relationships with co-workers and neighbors. Together these components explain about 70 percent of personal happiness. People who are happy don't get everything they want, but they want most of what they get. They also tend to stack the deck in their favor by choosing to cherish things that are within their grasp. People who find themselves depressed in life often set unreachable goals, setting themselves up to fail. Yet people who set high goals for themselves and reach them are no happier than people who set and reach more modest goals.

Whether you are assessing your position at work or your relationship with your family, don't begin with fantasy pictures of the world's richest person or the world's ideal family. Stay with reality and try to make things better, not perfect.

Improve for the Future

Spending your time imagining what would have been if you could have changed some little thing, some little decision in your life, is counterproductive. Think about how you can improve for the future, today, but don't waste your present time thinking about how you could have changed the past.

We could all trace our current position to every decision we have ever made. For example, where you sat in nursery school influenced who your friends were, which influenced what your interests were, which influenced how well you did in first grade, and so forth. You could ponder these things endlessly, but it wouldn't get you anywhere. Take a wrong turn on your way somewhere, and it won't pay to pull over and question why or how you took the wrong turn. What you need to do is think about how you can get from where you are to where you want to be. This same logic applies to your depression: Don't wallow in how much better everyone else's life is. Think about what you need to do to get where you want to be.

Research on athletes who came close to winning but lost in the Olympic finals found that those who spent the least amount of time thinking about how things might have ended differently were the most satisfied with their experience.

We'll be reviewing these concepts in the next several chapters, but let me introduce the final concept of Chapter 1—Claiming Your Life. We will then be ready to move on to your exercises for the first week.

Claiming Your Life

Think about the pioneers who traveled across the country with their families to start a new life. They found land and claimed it by hammering stakes in the ground; they marked their settlements and built their homes and *settled*. Do you feel settled in your life? Depression creates a type of blurriness that keeps you off center, off balance—as if you can't dig in and advance to where your dulled instincts know you can get to. You and I both know, however, that you are not here just to fill space, breathe air, and be in the background. Know this: It is likely that nothing would be the same if you did not exist. Everyone you have ever talked to, everyone who has ever seen you, every place you have ever been would likely be different if you didn't exist. We are all connected, and we are all affected by the decisions and even the existence of those around us.

Be Socially Open

Claim your life by claiming the important people in your life. They are just waiting for you to reach out to them. Depression can pull you far into yourself, and it leads you to believe that you might be a burden if you lean on others. This is just not true. Don't hold your thoughts, your worries, or your hopes inside of yourself. Share them with your friends and family. People who hold things inside tend to feel isolated, believing that others do not understand them. Those who share feel both supported and more content, even if the events and situations do not go exactly as they wish.

By sharing with others, you plug into the synergy of those around you who might be more optimistic and more motivated. Find these people; have them be support systems in your life. It will make a huge difference. And, then, when you are feeling better you will inspire others. We are all on this journey together, and we need to help each other.

The first line of business is to accept help. So imagine those people already in your life surrounding you right now, those people who are maybe a little farther down the path than you. They understand where you are and can offer you confidence, because they've already made some strides. You can join that group and you will, as we work day by day, in the moment, to strengthen your mind and your body.

The Building Blocks

Imagine for a moment that today is your last day on earth. Now, make a list of all the things that you feel you have accomplished, all the things that you are proud of, and all the things that make you happy. Is it your car? Your television? Your stereo? What's on the list of the fundamental elements of a satisfied life? Most people list their relationships with friends and family, the contributions they have made to others' lives, and the celebrated events of their life. Take some time to think about it and make a list.

It may be hard to come up with much at first, so if you draw a blank, don't worry. Just make a note to come back to this section in a week or two. It's just evidence of how your depression has you in lockdown mode.

When this loosens up, the light-filled memories will start to come through for you.

As you claim these fonder memories, and the relationships that have helped to compose them, you get to meet yourself again, and you start to take your life back. Claiming the successes of the past, and the important friends you have had (even if some of these relationships have stagnated during your depression), is reflective of a healthy you and the person you get to be again.

Many of us live as if the opposite were true. Instead of appreciating what is truly important and making that a priority, we collect material things and indicators of status or success without questioning just what success really means. The quality of your life is not necessarily based on what has happened or what you own. It's how you think about what you have and what has happened. There is no objective way to tell if you have had a good life, a good day, or a good hour. Your life is a success based solely upon your own judgment.

Claiming whatever is going right in your life is another useful mechanism for getting out of lockdown mode. Even if it's only your relationship with your cat that's going right at the moment, so be it. It counts as a positive. Your entire life doesn't hinge on one negative, overshadowing element. Your life is made up of many different facets. If you focus on the various aspects of your life you increase the chance of experiencing pleasure, even though one aspect of your life may be highly unsettled. Build your hopes on the many things that are important to you and allow yourself to benefit from the different things that contribute to your life. This is what it means to claim your life.

In Summary

Claiming your life also has a lot to do with keeping situations and relationships in perspective by seeing them through a compassionate, realistic lens. Satisfaction is relative. Your happiness is relative to a scale you have created for yourself. If you measure your satisfaction right now against the two or three greatest moments in your life, you will most likely be unhappy because those moments cannot be duplicated. If you measure today's satisfaction against some tough days you've had, you have all the reason in the world to appreciate this moment. Was today a good day? Well, what are you comparing it to?

My hope for you is that you open up a whole new world inside yourself and that you keep learning and growing. I heard this saying many years ago, and it stuck with me because at first I didn't understand what it meant: "The difference between the winners and the losers is the winners have lost more." As I mulled it over and over, I realized that what made people winners was their ability to not just tolerate losing but to learn from it. And eventually that learning curve got them to the winner's circle.

Are you ready to win at this depression match? It's you or it, so are you ready to bring your best game? I've just supplied you with loads of information about how to distinguish between depressed and healthy thinking and how to practice finding that healthier place and operating from there. I will be reviewing these concepts throughout the book, so don't worry if they haven't sunk in yet. Let's get moving.

Exercise Routine: Week One

Before beginning Week 1, be sure you have read the Introduction and Chapter 1.

Are you ready to get started? Regardless of how long it's been since you've exercised or what kind of physical shape you're in, I promise that most of you will be able to glide through Day One with nothing to fear. You might do the exercise and feel like it was too easy, feel tight in the beginning and looser at the end, dread it the whole way through, or feel exuberant as you finish. You also might feel sore later. Whatever happens, just remember: It won't hurt you. Even if you are sore, it means your muscles are working and your body is regrouping. So take a few deep breaths and focus on the moment.

Day One   1

Exercise time: 5 minutes
What you'll need: music, mat (optional), clock, towel, glass of water
Objectives: The objective of today is to be in your body in a powerful,

Photo1.1 Low-impact half jumping jacks

whole way even though you might feel emotionally oppressed (or weak) due to your depression. Yes, there is some gray matter in your brain that is not functioning properly, but all 206 bones in your body are okay, right? All 600-plus muscles that are attached to those bones are waiting for their turn to show up for you. You can do this. I believe in you (and, I'm only asking for five minutes).

Exercise: Put on some music and do five minutes of low-impact half jumping jacks.

Start position: Standing upright, shoulders back, stomach in, legs shoulder-width apart, arms at side.

With right foot, step sideways two to three feet (depending on how long your legs are) while simultaneously bringing your arms toward the ceiling. Your upper body mimics what it does in a jumping jack.

Return to start position and alternate the same half jumping jack stepping to the left while simultaneously bringing your arms up toward the ceiling. Move nice and easy.

Stop at five minutes.

Breathing pattern: Inhale as you move from the start position into the half jump and as you bring your arms up. Exhale as you move back to the start position.

When you begin the five minutes of low-impact side-lunge jumping jacks, go slowly so your muscles can stretch and warm up. Feeling resistant? That's okay; it's normal. But I hope you will allow me to do a little coaxing here: C'mon . . . (insert your name here), only five minutes. That's less time than it takes to get dressed. No need for fancy workout clothes; in fact you can do this barefooted. *You* make the commitment and don't let that depressed voice inside of your head talk you out of it. If not now, when?

Five minutes goes by fast, doesn't it? Welcome back! Want to do another five minutes? No? No worries, you have completed Day One. Congratulations! You have broken the spell. You know, that miserable, awful spell that keeps you sedentary because you don't have the energy to exercise and yet you don't have the energy because you're not exercising. I know this is not simply an issue of willpower. Just getting started is the first hurdle—it is truly the first challenge, and you've just overcome it.

If you answered, "Yes, I want to do more," fantastic! You rock! Try the side-lunge jumping jacks this time while making your mouth mimic a smile for as long as you can during the five minutes. *The most important factor right now is that you stay the course and take it one lunge at a time.* Right now we are simply setting attainable goals that will get you started little by little every day. Any goal that feels too overwhelming may tip your brain to follow your depression's advice to quit. And, by the way, by following through on this first exercise, you have made a responsible choice, implemented it, and made a deposit in your conviction bank. Great work.

Today's reflection: You can't control the speed of your recovery, but you can take small actions to remind yourself that you are a willing participant in this process. Each step you take is a step toward living more fully.

Homework: There is no homework today! Put the book in a special, noticeable place and we will continue tomorrow.

Day Two
2

Exercise time: 5–10 minutes
What you will need: music, mat (optional), clock, towel, glass of water
Objectives: How are those inner thigh muscles? Given that you don't walk sideways, you probably don't use them very much, and they are

whining. That's okay. The soreness just means they finally got to play and they just need to get a little more used to it. Continuing with the same workout will help move the soreness out of your muscles, so let's repeat the same workout, starting off slowly (which counts as your warm-up stretch), and picking up the pace in a measured way halfway through until the end.

Exercise: Before you begin today's physical exercise, I'd like to introduce you to the Challenge & Correct mental workout that you get to enjoy from this day forward. And I mean enjoy. It feels good to recognize that some rogue gray matter has been running the show and running you into the ground as a result. It feels good to corner *it* and give it a piece of *your* mind. You might want to practice some of the following comebacks: "Excuse me, but were you just bringing me down? I'm sorry, but I *do not* have time for that; I've got my life to live, so get lost!" or, "Back off, you are not in charge, I don't need your criticisms, and I am going to be my own hero. Like *now.*"

Today, we push through "its" Greatest Hits of Negative Blather by doing five minutes of low-impact half jumping jacks.

So, crank the music and practice your smile for two songs—that will be about five minutes of low-impact half jumping jacks. Can you do five more minutes? If not now, can you do it in five hours? Yes? Great! Set your alarm on your cell phone for five hours from now, to do five more minutes of low-impact half jumping jacks.

Today's reflection: So what junk has "it" been spinning today? When you woke up, did it say, "Ugh, let's stay in bed?" While you were brushing your teeth, did it tell you that the circles and bags under your eyes are getting worse? When getting dressed, did it comment that your clothes aren't fitting? The real problem is not your beauty or weight—it's that part of your brain that's doing the talking. But it does not compose *all* of your brain.

Have you had a physical in the last year? If not, the second piece of business today is to make that appointment. Self-care is so important and we need to be sure you are cleared for takeoff. Until then, we will continue to practice breaking its spell of inertia.

Homework: Start reading the first half of Chapter 2, so you will be ready for future weeks.

Day Three ———————————————— 3

Exercise time: 10 minutes

What you will need: music, mat (optional), clock, towel, glass of water

Objectives: Today's objective is to continue visualizing the power of your body supporting your depressed neurons. You have strength, even though your mind may be telling you otherwise. You can control your movements even though you can't yet control what is or is not happening in your brain (specifically, your synapses—the spaces between your neurons). Let your body be in charge and feel its willingness to show up for you.

Exercise: Put on some music and do five minutes of low-impact half jumping jacks. Rest for one minute, drink some water, keep the music rockin', and do five more minutes. Bravo!

Today's reflection: One of the things you can do while exercising (after you get the hang of the routine), is to practice dismantling and disarming negative self-talk. In "The 24-Hour Record" sidebar exercise on pages 11–12, you started to identify dysfunctional and stressful thoughts and perceptions. Now you're going to give your attention to changing some of those negative thoughts and perceptions. Although challenging situations in life cannot always be changed, your thoughts about them (and subsequently your feelings) can be changed. When distressed or depressed, our thoughts and perceptions can function like a lens through which we negatively interpret our self, our world, and the future. Look over the notes that you have taken about your depression. Do you see any patterns? Do any words show up repeatedly?

Homework: Start reading the second half of Chapter 2.

Day Four ———————————————— 4

Exercise time: 10 minutes

What you will need: music, mat (optional), clock, towel, glass of water

Objectives: Yesterday I asked you what words your depression uses repeatedly. Your objective during the exercise today is to name the words associated with your depression and then to think of the opposite word. For example, if a depression word is "down" then the opposite could be "up" or "boost" or "light." No need to get this perfect and tidy, any opposing words will do. Try to have some fun with it. Jot down the positive words in your notebook when you are done.

Exercise: Put on some music and do five minutes of low-impact half jumping jacks. Rest for one minute, drink some water, keep the music rockin', and do five more minutes.

Today's reflection: A word on commitment. Commitment is the foundation, the cement of any genuinely loving relationship with yourself and others. Commitments that are initially shallow may grow deep with time; if not, the relationship will likely fail or be sickly and weak. One of the risks of commitment is the fear of failure, but failure exists in the fear of the future, not "right now." Right now you can do something. You can simply commit to do things differently for now, and when "later" rolls around it will be right now again and you can recommit until your dedication deepens.

Dedication means you are willing to be personally challenged. Otherwise, you live in a state of your own entrapment, re-breathing your stale air, and enduring more and more of your mind's distortions. The tendency to avoid challenge is so common in humans it can almost be considered a characteristic of what it is to be human. But being natural does not mean it is essential or unchangeable. Most importantly, another characteristic of human behavior—perhaps the one that makes us tamer than our primate predecessors—is our capacity to do the unnatural, to rise above and transcend our own nature. All self-discipline might be defined as training ourselves to do the unnatural.

You are now more than halfway through the first week. Well done.

Homework: Start reading the first half of Chapter 3 so you will be ready for next week.

Day Five 5

Exercise time: 0–10 minutes

What you will need: music, mat (optional), clock, towel, glass of water

Objectives: Today's objective is to try to remember the positive "opposite" words that you brainstormed during your workout on Day Four. What were all those words? How many more positive words can you come up with during your exercise time?

Exercise: Put on some music and do five minutes of low-impact half jumping jacks. Rest for one minute, drink some water, keep the music rockin', and do five more minutes.

Today's reflection: A word about the TV. It robs you of time and never gives it back. Don't just turn on the TV because it's there and that's what you usually do. Turn it on only when there is something that you really want to watch. Your newly liberated hours can be spent doing more with your exercise plan and your mental health plan. Without TV, you can do something actively fun instead of passively distracting. Watching too much TV can triple your hunger for more possessions, while reducing your personal contentment by about 5 percent for every hour you watch per day.

Homework: Start reading the last half of Chapter 3 in preparation for Week Two.

Day Six — 6

Exercise time: 0–10 minutes (optional)

What you will need: music, mat (optional), clock, towel, glass of water

Objectives: Today's objective is to try to remember the positive "opposite" words that you brainstormed during your workout on Day Four. What were all those words? How many more positive words can you come up with during the exercise (if you decide to do it)?

Exercise: Put on some music and do five minutes of low-impact half jumping jacks. Rest for one minute, drink some water, keep the music rockin', and do five more minutes.

Today's reflection: To work out or not to work out today? That is the question. No matter which choice you make, just *make a choice*. You will most likely be okay with the consequences. In the case of exercise, the worst option is usually indecision. Today you have the option to rest. You don't really need the rest, as your exercises have been at a time limit that allows you plenty of rest from one day to the next. But I am setting up a pattern that you will maintain throughout the program. Eventually, a day of rest will be mandatory. If you are in a groove and want to continue, that's great. Regardless of what you decide, trust yourself enough to make this decision and then be honest with yourself about how you are feeling.

Write down any depressed thoughts and feelings that may come up.

Homework: Start reading the first half of Chapter 4 so that you are ready to go on Day One of Week 2. If you don't have a mat, consider purchasing one. It will come in handy during Week 2 and beyond. And it's a nice way to treat yourself for making the exercise commitment. Look at your decision to purchase a mat as adding to your conviction—and optimism.

Day Seven 7

Exercise time: 15 minutes

What you will need: music, mat (optional), clock, towel, glass of water

Objectives: As you are moving today, check in with your body and ask yourself, "Am I ready for more?" "Can I let myself get excited *and* also stay present with simply getting through the workout whether it is today or at Week 3?"

Exercise: Put on some music and do five minutes of low-impact half jumping jacks. Rest for one minute, drink some water, keep the music rockin', and do five more minutes. Rest for another minute, drink some water, keep the music rockin', and do the final five minutes.

Really excellent work! I'm glad you stayed with it and finished the week strong.

Today's reflection: Spread out good things over time. If you have 100 units of happiness for the year, it doesn't make sense to use them all up in one day and be miserable the other 364. For example, two gifts of $40 make people happier than a single $80 gift. What can you spread out over the day that will help you to feel satisfied at the end of the day? Maybe you could divide the time you spend on a crossword puzzle, for example. Do part in the morning, part after dinner, and the rest at bedtime. What are some other examples specific to your day-to-day life?

Homework: Start reading the last half of Chapter 4 for a smooth transition from Day Seven of Week One to Day One of Week 2.

Take a couple minutes to write a stream-of-consciousness comment about your week. The rule of stream-of-consciousness writing is that there are no rules. Any thoughts count. All feelings are important. Simply put pen to paper and see what you come up with.

_____

_____

_____

_____

_____

_____

_____

_____

2

Momentous Monumental Momentum!

You can think of the next several chapters as a process—you won't be just reading them but "doing" them. At times I will ask you to jot down some notes or pause to reflect and think about things differently. Bring a sense of adventure and curiosity to these pages. By doing these mental and physical exercises, you are building on developmental neural connections that were put into place in childhood, which you can deepen and refresh at any age.

First, I would like you to make a list of things that could cause you to put this book down at any given point during your reading sessions. I am going to call them "procrastination ponderings." You know, those nagging little things that suddenly seem so important as you think about starting your workout (folding the laundry, calling Aunt Sue, trimming your cuticles). Throughout the book you will see small charts with blank lines. Use these to jot down anything that is rummaging around in your head that could be a distraction. If you can't focus on the present moment, I can't help you to do the exercises that you need to do to feel better. Use these charts to write down what you need to do so that you'll remember to do them later.

Chart 2.1

Procrastination Ponderings

1. _____

2. _____

3. _____

4. _____

5. _____

I have structured this program to help you prevent your mood disturbances from blocking the very activities that will help you feel better. The assumption is that during this program, your depression *will* get in the way of naturally feeling like exercising. So, let's just count on that as a fact. It's better to count on it and be prepared or pleasantly surprised than to not expect it and be caught off guard and demoralized as a result. Throughout the book, I give you tips to make it easier to start the habit of regular exercise. I offer you ways of thinking about, scheduling, and monitoring your exercise program to help you stay motivated and on the benefits side of the equation. We're going to stack the deck in your favor so that your exercise routine gets easier and easier to fold into your day.

Getting to the Other Side

I consider it a privilege when people let me help them. And I certainly love it when they are successful. But as many success stories as there are, there are even more people who give up and never get to discover their potential. You know how to exercise. And you know how to eat right too. In fact, we are inundated with information about how to look and how to "be." This book is about your inside world, meaning, quite literally, your mind and your muscles. That is where all change begins. So how do you take that leap and join those who are on the other side, who are now thriving and not merely surviving?

Before I answer, you need to have a little heart-to-heart with yourself. As you have already noticed, this book is not just about learning the right exercises, it's about the big picture. It's about how to live the rest of your life by *not* letting depression run the show. Any discussion about getting into shape emotionally and physically is a discussion about how you have lived your life up to this point and how you want to live into a great future. Change always starts on the inside.

And that's where you have to look to answer the very first most important question: Have you made the decision to commit? You may have some intensely positive feelings about your commitment, you may still be ambivalent, or you may feel dread at the thought of it. Jot down all the various feelings you have about this question in Chart 2.2.

One of my all-time favorite quotes about commitment is attributed to Johann Wolfgang von Goethe: "Until one is committed there is hesitancy, the chance to draw back . . . The moment one definitely commits oneself, then Providence moves, too. All sorts of things occur to help one that would never otherwise have occurred. A whole stream of events issues from the decision, raising in one's favor all manner of unforeseen incidents and meetings and material assistance, which no man could have dreamed would have come his way. Whatever you can do, or dream you can do, begin it. Boldness has genius, power and magic in it. Begin it now."

Once you make your decision and know the reasons why you want to change, you find yourself endowed with a power that ignites the desire within you to reach your goals.

The second question is: What are your reasons for making this decision to commit to exercising your body and your mind? There is no right or wrong answer. As you jot down whatever comes to mind in Chart 2.2, be sure to capture the very first thing that pops into your mind, even if it doesn't quite make sense at the moment.

There is a big difference between daydreaming about something, deciding to do something, and having the conviction to actually do it. When you make the decision to change and you know your reasons, you will lasso the type of power that builds on the desire to make something happen.

Chart 2.2

Reasons for Committing

1. _____

2. _____

3. _____

4. _____

5. _____

6. _____

I don't know exactly what your reasons are, because they're as specific to you as your fingerprint. But following are some questions that can help you begin to find your own true reasons:

When you look at yourself, do you like what you see?
How do you truly feel about yourself, deep down inside?
Are you confident, spirited, and organized sometimes?, or hardly at all?
Do you often wonder if you're on the right track?

Now let's do some cost benefit analysis:

What is the cost of changing? Of staying where you are?
What are the benefits of changing? Of staying where you are?

In Chart 2.3, jot down whatever answers come to mind.

Did you find any real benefits to not changing? Or only costs? As you work through this chapter, continue to write down how much it has cost you and will continue to cost you to stay stuck. Now that your brain is engaged in this form of analysis, it will keep generating these costs. It is important to capture them, because we will be using them later in the program.

Chart 2.3

Cost Benefit Analysis

1. _____

2. _____

3. _____

4. _____

5. _____

6. _____

Your Personal GPS

Your everyday actions are directed by a type of conscious or unconscious future vision, which serves as your very own personal GPS. As you work through this program, you will be taking on newer, bigger, and more exciting challenges. You will be creating, modifying, and improving y our vision of your future. As a result, your everyday actions will naturally change.

When you develop a strong future vision, while staying in the present moment, you don't have to force yourself to set goals. Your mind unconsciously compels you to instinctively set them every day. And when you accomplish one of the goals, it's not the end but a starting point for another phase of the ongoing journey of your development, growth, and life.

What changes in your mind and body do you want to create within the next six to eight weeks? Be realistic, open, honest, and curious. Don't be concerned about what other people might want you to want or think. The things that surface in your mind, the things that bring up powerful feelings and get you excited about your future are what we're talking about here. *Your* dreams. Pick up a pen, think about them, and jot them down in Chart 2.4.

Chart 2.4

Changes in Your Mind and Body

1. _____

2. _____

3. _____

4. _____

5. _____

When you accomplish a goal, your dreams become even more inspiring, which then whets your appetite for more goals. When you begin the process of setting and achieving goals, you begin creating bigger dreams, which leads to greater optimism, a critical component for a healthy mindset. As you become more optimistic and confident with the program, goals will naturally surface and guide the way. So let go of future worry and hold onto a future full of hope; you will get there one step at a time.

The act of setting goals can take some practice, so here's a tip: Find someone who inspires you, someone who is a little further down the path than you are, and set your goals based on where he or she started out. Following is a list of famous people—musicians, astronauts, leaders, professional athletes—who have publically talked about their depression: Ashley Judd, Billy Joel, Boris Yeltsin, Brooke Shields, Buzz Aldrin, Delta Burke, Drew Carey, Emma Thompson, Harrison Ford, J. K. Rowling, Jim Carrey, Marie Osmond, Mike Wallace, Olivia Newton-John, Rosie O'Donnell, Sheryl Crow, Terry Bradshaw. You may want to find out how some or all of them worked through it. It's a great place to start because that person is living proof that it can be done.

Once you create your list of goals, hang on to it, and read it in the morning when you get up and again at night before you go to bed, every day. Recite them aloud, as if you were describing your own future to somebody else. Speak with total conviction and bubbliness. Remove any doubt from your tone of voice. Picture each one as something you absolutely will accomplish. Say so with outright confidence. Remember, hope and optimism are not strong enough emotions to create the desire you'll need to keep going. You must have growing conviction that what your imagination has created can truly be your future life. View this as an exciting journey that you are embarking upon. Don't feel bubbly or convinced? Remember: Fake it till you make it.

Using Your Body to Help Your (Sometimes Resistant) Mind

Mind and body are connected, and in this program, you are intervening with your body to help your mind and mood. Exercise keeps you focused on doing, moving, and achieving and helps you establish healthy patterns of activity and rest. This program helps you give your body what it needs to balance your mind and emotions.

Depression is characterized by self-perpetuating cycles of low activity or avoidance, so it is important to make the argument for exercise a strong one. Memorize the following argument and keep it in your proverbial back pocket, as I tell my patients: Exercise works in part because it returns the body to adaptive action, a condition in which your muscles have to adapt to what you are asking of them. Rising to this adaptive challenge increases feelings of competency and pride and your ability to stave off negative mood states. As you learn more about your feelings, the meaning of some of your negative or irrational emotions will change. As you stay active despite low moods, these episodes of low moods should decrease.

Exercise can also have some powerful effects on how you interpret the physiological experience of emotion. When you fear bodily symptoms, they take on a life of their own and can become more difficult to tolerate. Exercise can reduce the fears surrounding these anxiety sensations. It can be used to help you feel less pushed around by some of the harder feelings you may experience.

Even if you are already sold on the fact that regular exercise is good for your mood and body, it can be hard to start, *particularly* when you are feeling down. Remember: The assumption is that during this program, your depression *will* get in the way of naturally feeling like exercising. We are going to count on that for a fact, so that you are prepared for your resistance if it rears its head, or pleasantly surprised if it doesn't. Over time, exercise becomes the "go-to" activity that you do precisely because you *want* to feel a lift. The fact that you get into good shape and take on healthier ways of nourishing yourself in the process is an extra benefit.

When Life Gets in the Way

Everyday life situations, conflicts, and unexpected distractions can interfere with your best intentions. Many of these obstacles are often predictable, understandable, and preventable. So let's identify two situational problems that can interfere with establishing an exercise pattern, discuss the best time of day to exercise, and then plan some intervention strategies to keep you on track.

Ambivalence

Given that we know that strong motivation alone is not enough to create a behavior change, you will need to play it smart and "do" rather than "stew." Don't stew about whether "to exercise" or "not to exercise;" just make the decision to do it. Exercising one or more times establishes the inward desire to do it again. The strong desire to exercise most likely will not come until after you have successfully altered your mood through exercise, so don't waste your time waiting for it. I use the word altered because sometimes when you exercise you may feel a lift, and other times you might get in touch with an intense feeling that isn't necessarily exuberant. You will feel more "alive," however, which is better than feeling like you have been knocked down and can't get up.

Your Home Is Not Exercise Friendly

It is crucial to make new habits easy to start and maintain rather than just hope everything will fall into place. Your feelings of conviction and motivation are dependent on your external environment as well as your mood. So establish an exercise area in your home, whether it's a mat you place on the bedroom floor or an entire level of your home. The more you arrange the conditions in your environment to make it easier to exercise, the more you naturally feel like doing it.

Instead of focusing on exercise as a vague, generic concept, simply focus on the next step. Put yourself in a position where putting on your workout clothes and picking up the dumbbells is easy and accessible. Perhaps you could put the clothes on the arm of the couch and the dumbbells on the floor next to the couch. When you wake up, or get home from work (whichever part of the day you pick), your first step is to simply put on your clothes, and the next step is to pick up the dumbbells.

The Argument for Morning Exercise

If you are a morning person, this timeframe should be a good fit for your exercise routine. You will enjoy the sense of accomplishment that comes with mastering your goal first thing in the morning. The post-workout shower becomes your regular shower. It's typically a distraction-free time, so there are fewer chances of being disrupted. In the same vein, it becomes your personal quiet time.

For some people, the biggest challenge with a morning workout is getting out of bed earlier than usual. If you stay up a little too late or are not a morning person, you are likely to talk yourself into hitting the snooze button on the alarm clock. If you want to do the morning routine, before you go to bed, affirm your decision to do a morning workout. And when you wake up, do "the robot." Don't think. Don't feel. Just "do." Execute the program. When robots are programmed they don't talk back. They don't say, "Just five more minutes of snooze time," or "I will do it this evening." Expecting your resistant reaction will help you roll with your plan in the morning. Having the "robot talk" with yourself the night before may even bring a smile to your face and a slight smugness about having defeated the resistant, uncooperative voice of depression.

The Argument for Afternoon Exercise

If you have a flexible daytime schedule or a long enough lunch break at work, afternoon exercise is an extremely effective way of de-stressing your mind and freeing your body of accumulated negative energies. Afternoon exercise can break the monotony at the workplace and permit your body to rejuvenate naturally. While afternoon exercise may leave you slightly fatigued, your mind will be ready to accept new challenges with ease.

You will need to do "the robot" in the afternoon, as well, because the distracted, anxious part of your brain will be telling you that you have too much to do: "Just one more thing," or "I really should make this phone call first," or "This e-mail will only take me a second." Make the appointment with yourself to take some midday time to recharge your tired batteries.

As you become more and more accountable for your health, you begin to realize that you can boost your productivity by managing your mood and stress through exercise.

The Argument for Evening Exercise

Another excellent way to unwind is to exercise when you get home from work, up to three hours before bedtime. Evening exercise should ideally be seen as a suitable way of de-stressing from work or school and facing your family with a smiling face. Again, establishing a strategy is imperative, or you may be tempted to skip your workout because of fatigue, the weather, evening plans, or errands. In a nutshell, that resistant voice may be chattering on, distracting you in one way or another.

Remember your commitment to yourself and make a serious effort to integrate it into your family routine; think of it as literally leaving the residue of work behind you. When you are finished, take some time to analyze the positive effect of your workout session. A shower and change of clothes after exercising helps you prepare for a peaceful evening at home.

Other Tips

Purchase a workout outfit that you like. This allows you to treat yourself and adds to your conviction. Many discount stores have active wear, so find some comfortable, supportive clothing and sneakers. Music makes it all a lot more fun, too. Or you can download an audio book into your smart phone, plug it into some speakers, and voilà, you are adding another benefit to how you are spending your time. A number of local programs might be available to support your new habits. USA FIT is a commercial exercise support network that might be in your region; it provides a training program for specific events including coaching, support, and networking with fellow fitness folks. Two good sites for connecting with others and learning different ideas about how to make it all work are www.mapmyrun.com and www.fitlink.com.

Mental Momentum Leads to Physical Results and Vice-Versa

Now that you're geared up mentally, let's detail your strength-training program. Continue going over the next two chapters so you can learn about the amazing things your body will be doing for you.

The human body is the most sophisticated example of integrated functioning that exists on this planet—light-years beyond the most sophisticated technology. Are you willing to simply (emphasis on the simply) get better? No special materials are necessary except the dumbbells. You already possess all that you need in your own being and in the palm of your hands.

Chapter 3 leads you through the strength training part of your routine, which you will schedule into one day per week. Chapter 4 goes over aerobic options, which you will schedule into the remaining five days of a week. One day of each week should be free of exercise.

I have prepared charts for you to use to schedule your workouts and track your feelings, as you work on healing your depression day by day. Chart 2.5 is a sample of an exercise chart for the second week.

You'll start using these charts in Chapter 4, after I've introduced you to the Move More, Smile More strength-training routine.

	Day 1 Date: T	Day 2 Date: W	Day 3 Date: Th	Day 4 Date: F	Day 5 Date: Sa	Day 6 Date: Su	Day 7 Date: M
Chart 2.5			**Sample Week**				
Time of day	1 pm	10 am	4 pm	10 am	10 am	4 pm	8 am
Type of exercise	MMSMR (strength training)	Rest day, but still wanted to walk	Biked	Brisk walk	Swimming	Biked	Brisk walk
Intensity (easy-hard)	Moderate	Easy	Hard overall	Hard	Middle of the road	Hard	Moderate to hard
How long?	35 min.	30 min.	40 min.	30 min.	20 min.	45 min.	20 min.
Pre-exercise mood	Hopeful	Numb	Eager	Numb	Scared	Positive	Tired, grumpy
Post-exercise mood	Relieved, proud,	Relaxed	Happy!	Energized	Tentative	Really positive – YAY ME!	Glad I did it!
Music, TV, other notes	Played Tyro Cruz CD, remember towel tomorrow	Listened to Martha Stewart podcast	Tried to remember opposite, positive words. Will keep trying…	Listened to Ipod	Haven't swam in long time, felt good to move, very self-conscious	Bring Gatorade instead of water next ride	Pushing through worked! Play dance music next walk

3

The Move More, Smile More Routine

Now we're going to step it up just a notch, and I'm guessing you're ready for it, as your body is more limber and your muscles are primed. Following is a strength-building workout I have designed that works every major muscle group. I will refer to this part of the workout program as the Move More, Smile More Routine (MMSMR). You will be doing this workout one day per week, then you will have a day without any exercise, then you will do a cardio exercise (such as brisk walking, hiking, biking, swimming, and so forth) on the next five days of the week.

Why have strength or resistance training as part of the plan? Strength training protects bone health and muscle mass, makes you stronger and fitter, and helps you develop better body mechanics. But perhaps most important of all, it boosts energy levels and improves your mood, by elevating your level of endorphins (natural opiates produced by the brain), which make you feel great. The MMSMR includes compound exercises, which are designed to simultaneously work multiple muscle groups, and simple exercises that isolate one or two muscles at a time. There are only eight exercises in the whole workout.

A Note about Weights

In order to make your muscles stronger, you will be using your own weight as resistance as well as using dumbbell weights. You'll need a set of dumbbells, starting with either two or five pounds up to twenty pounds, depending on your prior activity levels over the past year. It may take several workouts with different weights and exercises before you settle on the perfect weight for you. But then, you will be good to go.

Studies show that strength training helps with depression when subjects increase the weight they lift over time. This means that using the same weight for weeks and weeks and lifting it over and over won't create the necessary changes over the long run. You need dumbbells of varying weights to keep your muscles challenged as they get stronger and need more resistance. Studies measuring the effects of exercise on depression using successful strength training programs have several things in common. These factors include warming up first before using weights and working the major upper and lower body muscles.

In the beginning, even if you're in shape, pick a weight where you reach muscle failure, a deep state of muscle fatigue, by about the eighth repetition. This may take some trial and error. Start with a low weight and work your way up until you find the weight that fits the bill.

When I use the word repetition, or "rep," I am referring to the motion of moving the weight or your body both up and down. For example, if you started with the dumbbells at your side and lifted them using your forearm (bending your elbow) toward your shoulder, touching your shoulder with the weight and bringing it back down to your side, and you did this full motion ten times, you would have done ten reps of a bicep curl.

Keep Focused

Your mind might start wandering right now and you might be starting to feel slightly anxious. That is normal. You are about to learn and embark upon a new routine, so bear with this process and don't abandon yourself. If you are distracted by thoughts that are making you want to put this book down and go do something else, use Chart 3.1 to make a note of them—we will get to them later.

```
Chart 3.1
                    Procrastination Ponderings

1. _____

2. _____

3. _____

4. _____

5. _____
```

Following are some important things to focus on during the first few times you do this routine:

- The smooth movement of your body
- Your breathing
- Getting comfortable with what it feels like to reach muscle failure
- Pushing beyond muscle failure
- Relaxing

Muscle failure refers to the point at which you can no longer move the weight without altering proper form. When you reach this point, your muscles sustain tiny micro-fiber tears that rebuild themselves as you rest. As the muscles heal, they come back stronger than ever before, regardless of your age. This is necessary so that your body can handle future weight loads with more ease.

For your first workout, take any reasonable looking weight and start your set. You may crank right past eight reps to ten or more. Or you may not be able to go past four. For your next workout, adjust accordingly. After a few workouts, you will know which weight to use to get to eight reps before reaching failure. From there, you will start measuring regular progress.

Stick with an approximate eight-rep count until you're feeling comfortable and confident with the program. What matters the most is good form, consistent rhythm, and that you take yourself to muscle failure and beyond.

Speaking of form, let's have a thorough tutorial on the correct way to do the MMSMR—or any weight-lifting program, for that matter.

Proper Form

The routine does not take long, but it must be done correctly in order for it to work. You move your body, or your weights, in a way that makes each muscle in your body dig deep to pull it all together and make the exercise work. You want to do the routine in seven- to ten-second rhythms: up for seven to ten seconds and then down for seven to ten seconds. Don't stop at the top or the bottom. Maintain consistency so that your muscles sustain a continuous and steady weight load. Doing the exercises in a slow, methodical manner is challenging, which builds greater strength and makes for a more efficient workout.

Throughout the entire exercise session, make sure that you breathe, focus, and relax. Breathe through every rep slowly but surely, focus on the muscles you are working, and relax knowing that you have everything in control. Breathing too quickly causes strain on your body's organs and increases your blood pressure, which isn't what you want. Breathe in and out slowly so that you can maintain a steady heart rate. Don't tighten up the other body parts or muscles that are not being used during any given part of the workout. Your face can't lift that dumbbell, so there's no use scrunching it all up in a knot. Maintain a zenlike focus on the muscles that you are working out and don't let your focus drift away to anything else.

Aches and Pains

When you reach muscle fatigue and cause your muscle cells to tear, you feel sore. This is "good pain" caused by the tiny tears in the muscle sheaths that rebuild themselves between your strength training workouts. Remember, as the muscles heal, they come back stronger than ever before. The MMSMR targets all of your most important muscles so that you start working and rebuilding them vigorously. During just a single workout, you will be able to work all of those important muscles. Once you've pushed through your first workout, you will take a five- to seven-day rest from weight lifting.

MMSMR Exercises

Before doing the Move More, Smile More Routine, read through the description of each exercise so you have an idea of what it involves. You will begin the actual routine in Week 2 (Chapter 4).

1. Lateral pulldown/forward lunge
Start position: Standing upright with normal posture, neck relaxed, feet shoulder-width apart, stomach in, arms extended straight up holding your dumbbells, palms pointing toward the ceiling.

Exercise: With right foot, lunge forward (making sure knee does not go past big toe) while simultaneously pulling dumbbells down (treat

Photo 3.1: Lateral pulldown/forward lunge

dumbbells as if they are a lateral pulldown bar) so that there is a 90-degree angle at your elbow.

Go back to start position and alternate same lunge/pulldown using left foot. It will take you a few times to get your balance, so the slower the better.

Continue alternating until you reach muscle failure in either your arms or legs. *Sometimes muscle failure is not at the point where you cannot lift the weight any longer but occurs at a point where you are pulling out of the correct form to accomplish the exercise.* If this is happening, hold where you are, continuing to contract your muscles for a ten-count and then return to the start position and move on to the next exercise.

Breathing pattern: Inhale as you move from the start position into the lunge and as you bring the dumbbells down. Exhale as you move back to the start position.

2. Half jumping jacks with dumbbell

This is the same exercise that you did the first week (see page 25), only now you will be adding a little resistance to the upper body portion of the movement by using dumbbells.

Start position: Standing upright, shoulders back, stomach in, legs shoulder-width apart, arms at side with dumbbell (weight ranging from two to twelve pounds).

Exercise: With right foot, step sideways two to three feet (depending on how long your legs are) while simultaneously bringing your arms toward the ceiling. Your upper body mimics what it does in a jumping jack.

Return to start position and alternate same half jumping jack stepping to the left while simultaneously bringing your arms up toward the ceiling. Move nice and slow.

Stop when you reach muscle failure.

Breathing pattern: Inhale as you move from the start position into the half jump and as you bring the dumbbells up. Exhale as you move back to the start position.

3. Side-lunge using dumbbell or medicine ball

Start position: Standing in left lunge position with left leg three feet from right, knee bent where knee does not extend over left toe. Dumbbell (two to twelve pounds) or medicine ball (five to eight pounds) is positioned over left knee.

Photo 3.2: Side-lunge using dumbbell or medicine ball

Exercise: Shift weight to right foot while raising weight or ball from left knee up and over right shoulder, stand on right foot, and lift left foot off ground. Return to start position and repeat until you reach muscle failure.

Rest for one minute.

Do another set starting in a right-side lunge position.

Breathing pattern: Inhale as you move from the start position into the lunge, as you are bringing the dumbbells up. Exhale as you move back to the start position.

4. Upper Abdominals

Start position: Lying face up on the floor, knees bent and separated, feet flat on the floor, separated and lined up with your hips, arms placed behind your head or folded across your chest.

Exercise: Push your lower back flat into the floor through the entire exercise. Hold your stomach in tight. Lift your chest until your upper abs are fully contracted and your shoulders are about four to six inches off the floor. Keep your neck and head straight. (Be careful not to tuck your chin into your chest as you lift. Do not pull on your neck, keep your arms in the same flat position throughout.)

Photo 3.3: Upper abdominals

Reverse the motion, lowering yourself back to the floor, but stop just before touching your shoulders or head to the floor.

Do not rest until you reach muscle failure.

Breathing pattern: Exhale as you move from the start position of one rep and inhale as you move back to the start position for the next rep.

5. Lower Abdominals

Start position: Lying flat on the floor, legs and heels pointing toward the ceiling, arms at your side, palms pointing downward. I call these reverse sit-ups.

Exercise: Keeping your hands on the floor, let your lower abdominal muscles pull your butt and pelvis 1–2 inches off the floor. (As these muscles get stronger, you will rely less on your hands to brace yourself against the floor.) Hold at the top for three seconds and gradually lower your bottom until it touches the floor.

Repeat entire motion until you reach muscle failure. The slower you do this one, the sooner you reach muscle failure. As with any of these exercises, the more you do them, the easier they get.

Breathing pattern: Exhale as you move from the start position of one rep and inhale as you move back to the start position for the next rep.

Photo 3.4: Lower abdominals

6. Back extensions

Start position: Lying face down on the floor with both arms extended straight out ahead of you.

Exercise: Lift your shoulders/arms and legs off the floor simultaneously, pivoting at your waist. Hold at the top for a three-second squeeze then release downward. Keep your muscles contracted and do not rest at the bottom.

Repeat until you reach muscle failure. Given the limited range of motion, you will not be counting any reps going up or coming down, just

Photo 3.5: Back extensions

do the exercise slowly; you will get better and better at this one as time goes on.

Breathing pattern: Exhale as you move from the start position of one rep and inhale as you move back to the start position of the next rep.

7. "Glute" crunches

Start position: Lying face up on the floor, arms at your sides, feet 18–24 inches apart. Your feet are drawn toward your waist, knees in the air. Your butt is lifted off the floor forming a relaxed "dip" at your waist.

Exercise: Tighten your glutes (the muscles in your butt) and straighten the dip, as if you are trying to touch the ceiling with your belly button. At the end position, your glutes should be contracted as tightly as possible. Hold the squeeze for three seconds and then relax. The movement of your torso from taut to relaxed is subtle—you are not lowering your butt more than three inches from the point of greatest contraction. Again, slow and measured gets you to muscle failure the quickest.

Breathing pattern: Exhale as you tighten and raise and inhale as you relax and lower.

Photo 3.6: Glute crunches

8. Bicep curl

Start position: Standing upright with good posture (stomach sucked in, shoulders back), your feet somewhat wider than shoulder width with knees slightly bent, dumbbells held at your side, palms facing your hips.

Exercise: Raise the right weight to your right shoulder. Only your forearm should move, rotating at your elbow as you raise the weight. (Swinging the dumbbell reduces the effectiveness of the lift. You can avoid this by keeping your elbows at your sides throughout each repetition.)

Return the weight to the starting position in a controlled manner, keeping tension on your biceps throughout the lift.

Raise the left weight to the left shoulder.

Do the same number of reps on each side. Stop when you reach muscle failure.

Breathing pattern: Exhale as you lift the weight and inhale as you lower the weight on each side.

9. Tricep kick backs

Start position: Standing with your feet somewhat wider than shoulder-width apart, knees slightly bent, dumbbells in hand, elbows cocked back as high as possible, pointing toward the ceiling.

Photo 3.7: Bicep curl

Exercise: Grip the dumbbells so that your palms face your sides. Slowly extend both your arms back until they are as straight as they will go (do not change the position of your elbow) and then lower your arms back to the starting position.

Your upper arms and elbows should not move at all during the entire set. This is very important: If you can't do a complete set without moving your upper arms and elbows, use a lighter weight. Keep your elbows as high as possible throughout.

Do as slowly and as measured as possible until you reach muscle failure.

Breathing pattern: Exhale as you extend your arms and inhale as you move back to the start position.

Let's Review

The strength-building workout is for your entire body—upper and lower, back and front. During the lateral pull-down/forward lunge, the half jumping jacks with dumbbell, and the side-lunge using dumbbell or medicine ball you'll be working more than one muscle group simultaneously. The other exercises focus on just one or two muscles concurrently. In this program, you will work your entire body through a total of eight exercises. When you begin, choose a weight that will give you trouble doing more than eight reps. It will take a few workouts to determine the perfect weight for each exercise.

As you do the exercises, focus on your breathing and form. Breathe slowly, focus on what you are doing, and start growing accustomed to pushing past your comfort level. It will be difficult at first. Find your comfort level with each workout, and push beyond it—even if it's just a single rep. Stick with that same rep count for the following couple of workouts until you become confident in that routine. And so on.

Your muscles are engaged (or contracted) the whole time when performing your reps. Don't worry about the number of reps you are doing; you will have a sense if it's too few or too many. Simply focus on the quality of your performance. You need to get used to the proper form throughout the entire rep for the exercise to do its magic on your muscles. It may seem difficult at first, but as you continue to practice, it will begin to feel like second nature.

As the weeks go by, your failure rep will start being at nine, ten, and then even eleven reps. This is good because it means you are getting stronger. When you reach this point, it's time to start adding more weight so that you have to go back to just doing seven or eight reps.

Remind yourself that when you reach failure, your body will inform you that it needs rest. You'll feel that burn, then keep pushing for just a few seconds more.

Embrace Failure

When you get to your last rep, you need to be able to make it through another ten seconds to be completely finished. This very last push is commonly referred to as the failure rep because many people give up at the last minute. Your muscles are already giving out, weakening to the point that you feel as if you can't make it another second. But, you need to think about the benefits that you reap from those last ten seconds of that last rep.

Every time you reach that last rep, for several weeks, you are going to feel as if you can't keep pushing. You will feel as though you really need to stop because of how uncomfortable it is. Keep pushing. After those first several weeks, it will become natural, and you'll have no problem pushing yourself to the absolute maximum. You will get used to it, and you will feel better about yourself, not just physically, but also mentally. When you finish that last ten seconds of the last rep, slowly and consistently let the weight down. Don't let it down quickly or drop it, you want to avoid injuries at all cost. Maintain the same speed and control that you had throughout the other reps.

There is a "before and after" experience to this style of strength training. Once you have experienced pushing or holding your position for another ten seconds even though your muscle is exhausted, you will never want to go back to any namby-pamby type of strength training again. Your thoughts on how you work out completely change. You feel powerful afterward. Remember this feeling.

The eight strength-building exercises are just what your body needs— no more and no less. They are just enough to turn the switch on for your muscles to begin the rebuilding process. Eight exercises of about two minutes each equals a fifteen-minute exercise regimen. It is important that you don't stop between each exercise. Just keep going, keep pushing. You will be gradually moving your muscles and joints rather than forcefully moving them, which means that your joints aren't harmed, as they might be when you perform aerobic activities.

The Importance of Rest

I've touched on the concept of rest, but I haven't mentioned how important it is. In terms of exercise, rest is defined as the recovery period after a completed training session. The body reacts to the strength training by increasing its ability to cope with the weights as your muscles regroup on rest day; rest is crucial if you want to build a strong and fit body.

You could compare the importance of rest to the importance of having oxygen to breathe or nutrients to keep your body moving. You use rest to recover from exercises. During your exercises, you significantly "break down" your muscles. Rest prevents you from irritating the muscle cells before they've been able to repair themselves. Rest is an integral part of the exercise and weight-training process and allows the muscle cells to start their natural repair process. You get to rest while the cells do the strengthening work for you.

Not resting between workouts leads to the following conditions:

Lack of energy (eventually chronic fatigue)
Slow metabolism
Weakened immune system
Muscle strains

The strength-building portion of MMSMR requires you to refrain from lifting weights for five or six days. Aside from rest, proper nutrition (covered in Chapter 5) is also essential.

Aerobic Training (aka, The Cardio Plan)

Aerobic exercise is also a key component to alleviating depression symptoms. You are doing aerobic, or "cardio," training if you can perform an exercise that elevates your normal heart rate and gets your pulse to a level that is more than half of your maximum heart rate. To figure out your maximum heart rate, subtract your age from 220; this is the maximum number of times your heart should beat per minute.

A rule of thumb for knowing whether you are in your best heart-rate zone is as follows: If you can effectively carry on a conversation with someone while exercising, you are not participating in aerobics because your heart rate isn't high enough. If it were, you couldn't carry on a conversation. You would be breathing hard, which is exactly what you need to be doing. However, you should not be gasping for your next breath the entire time.

Many people ask me, What is the best type of aerobic exercise? The answer is simple: walking. It is something that we do on a daily basis and we are made to do. It is a perfect exercise for the treatment of depression.

How Much?

One question that may be on your mind in terms of how to use exercise as therapy is: How much should I do? There is no firm answer—especially given depression's wide spectrum of symptoms and severity—but researcher Madhukar Trivedi has drawn some conclusions about the amount necessary to be effective. By quantifying exercise as a dose, he hopes to cast treatment in terms the medical profession might accept.

In one study, Trivedi and Andrea Dunn divided eighty depressed patients into five groups, four with exercise protocols of different intensities and frequencies and one control group assigned to supervised stretching only (to see if social interaction with the supervisors had any effect). They used calories burned per pound of weight as the "dose" measure. The high-intensity groups burned an average of 1,400 calories (eight calories per pound) during the course of either three or five sessions per week.

At the end of three months, regardless of frequency, the high-intensity groups cut their depression scores in half. The low-intensity groups burned an average of 560 calories (3 calories per pound) and lowered their scores by one-third, about the same as the stretching group—and about as effective as a placebo.

What this means for you is that moderate exercise will suffice but more intense exercise is even better. I expect that you will pace yourself and build to a greater intensity level as the weeks go on, so don't feel overwhelmed (remember our discussion about setting attainable goals). This information just helps to set some parameters for you.

By now, you've already scheduled your doctor appointment for a full medical evaluation. It's important to be aware of any physical conditions that could limit your participation in the exercises contained in this book. Let your physician know that you are about to start an exercise program that is targeting the public health recommended dose for adults from the American College of Sports Medicine.

In addition to getting your physician's approval, you need to pay attention to your body and work out at your own level, advancing according to your body's abilities. There is a difference between soreness (good pain) and having an injury. You should not be experiencing shooting pain anywhere in your body while in a resting state. Be sure to talk with your doctor if you have any breathing difficulties, chest pain, dizziness, joint pain, or high blood pressure. Even with these conditions, this program might be fine for you, but the decision should be made as a collaboration between you and your physician.

For the Mathematicians

Trivedi and Dunn based the high dose on public health recommendations for exercise, which suggest thirty minutes of moderate aerobic activity on most days, depending on your weight, metabolism, and type of exercise. If you weigh 150 pounds, your dose would translate into three hours of moderate intensity per week. The low dose would be equivalent to eighty minutes per week.

To figure out how many calories you should be burning for the high dose per week, multiply your body weight by eight. Then head to the gym to find out how many calories you burn during a given workout (most aerobic machines track this for you). If you weigh 150 pounds and burn 200 calories in thirty minutes on the elliptical trainer, you'd want to do six sessions a week (200 x 6 = 1,200 calories) to meet the 1,200 calorie (8 x 150) high dose.

4

Week Two — Creating Your Personalized Action Plan

You're probably tired of me telling you what to do. This chapter walks you through how to solidify your personalized exercise plan. My hope is that you will be getting used to exercise as being a part of the "norm" of your week, so that it will become an "I can't live without it" activity—a critical part of the formula for your quality of life equation.

The first task at hand is for you to continue to capture the positive feelings coming from exercising and to harness them into each subsequent workout. Chart 4.1 will help you to take an inventory of your first week of exercise: What felt good to you? What didn't? Did certain times of the day work better than others? Did music help? Write down everything you can think of. There are no wrong answers here.

Write out a tentative exercise plan for Week 2 in Chart 4.2. You will be firming this up at the end of the chapter. For now, plug in when you think you might be able to exercise and what exercises you would like to do each day.

Next, take an inventory of the thoughts that arise when you think about exercising during this second week—any thoughts, including those of resistance, procrastination, and sabotage, as well as cautious or hopeful thoughts. Note them in Chart 4.3.

Chart 4.1	Week One						
	Day 1 Date:	Day 2 Date:	Day 3 Date:	Day 4 Date:	Day 5 Date:	Day 6 Date:	Day 7 Date:
Time of day							
Type of exercise							
Intensity (easy-hard)							
How long?							
Pre-exercise mood							
Post-exercise mood							
Music, TV, other notes							

Chart 4.2	Week Two (Guess-timate)						
	Day 1 Date:	Day 2 Date:	Day 3 Date:	Day 4 Date:	Day 5 Date:	Day 6 Date:	Day 7 Date:
Time of day							
Type of exercise							
Intensity (easy-hard)							
How long?							
Pre-exercise mood							
Post-exercise mood							
Music, TV, other notes							

Chart 4.3

Thoughts about Exercising

1. _____

2. _____

3. _____

Potential Problems or Barriers

1. _____

2. _____

3. _____

Solutions or Alternatives

1. _____

2. _____

3. _____

Congratulations. You just got started on claiming your unique plan. Did you know that you have a running dialogue in your head that generates about fifty thousand thoughts a day? Knowing what the depressed part of your brain is jabbering about is critical. It helps you to know when it's time for the constructive part of your brain to intervene.

This chapter describes the cardio portion of your week. Included are a few different exercise types that vary in intensity. You may prefer to do cardio exercises that are not on this list, and that's fine. You choose which type is best for you. I recommend that you take it slow the day after your

Chart 4.4

Procrastination Ponderings

1. _____

2. _____

3. _____

4. _____

5. _____

6. _____

7. _____

full-body MMSMR workout and then alternate light- and moderate-intensity activities each day, with one high-intensity day thrown in as you feel up to it. After assembling the plan, record in the appropriate column how you are feeling just before exercising, how you felt just after, and again just before going to bed.

Before I introduce the cardio exercises, I would like to talk to you about the pact you are making with yourself—the agreement you are making with yourself to get better.

Just in case your unconscious (or conscious) mind is saying, "Uh-oh, more serious, lecture-type stuff that will stir me up. Maybe I should make a list of what I need to get at the grocery store instead . . .," go ahead and make a few notes about those ponderings in Chart 4.4, and then your mind will be clear for the discussions that follow.

Keeping Your Word with Yourself

In Chapter 2, you made a list of your goals; go ahead and review them before continuing to read this section.

Goals are only as good as the words you use to describe them. You see, your word is your commitment to yourself. It is an important promise that you need to make to yourself; but don't just make it—keep it. In order to

---

Chart 4.5
Memories of Unintentionally Letting Yourself Slide

1. _____

2. _____

3. _____

4. _____

5. _____

6. _____

7. _____

---

have true confidence in yourself, you must trust yourself. You develop self-trust by finishing what you start and by doing what you tell yourself you're going to do. This includes your commitment to start an exercise regimen.

Think about it: Would you trust someone who was always caught fibbing? Or maybe someone who never abided by the rules? You would just figure they are full of hot air and that even if you could trust them sometimes, you never know which time that will be, so you never take their word very seriously.

You can't get away with leading yourself on. It's not as if you are someone on the other side of the conversation who has no idea whether you are telling the truth or not—you *do* know. Sure, you can ignore the essence of the appeasement without action, but eventually, deep down, the truth is hiding and is eating away at your inner self.

A strong, healthy mind creates a strong, healthy body and vice-versa. That is a fact. When I see men and women who are depressed and out of shape, I see lives not fully lived, and I see a loss of potential. I think people need someone to help them realize that they can feel better and look better. Your body is the epicenter of your universe. You go nowhere without it. It is truly the temple of your mind and your soul. Do you think that maybe slowly, gradually, without being aware of it, you gave up? Do you remember when this erosion first began? Jot down whatever comes to mind in Chart 4.5.

Whether you realize it or not, a lot of your life challenges may stem from a lack of self-trust and honor. Many of us find this hard to face, but self-trust is something we need to meet straight on. You are lying to yourself when you know that you aren't doing something you promised yourself you'd do. For example, eating healthier, exercising on a regular basis, finishing a fitness schedule, and so on. After a stretch of telling yourself you are going to do something and then not doing it, you will notice that your overall mood, confidence, and self-trust start to head south. You begin to feel a nagging sense of emptiness, which leads to bigger issues such as uncertainty and low morale. You've been down that road and you don't need to go there again. The good news is that you don't have to. You don't have to feel empty forever. If you slip and revisit empty-land, know that it is possible to lift your spirits and get back up again.

The Truth Shall Set You Free

While it may seem hard to believe at first, take it from me: It's easier to stay true to yourself and to keep your promises than it is to break your word. When you keep a promise to yourself, the amount of energy as well as future potential that is released is remarkable. Remember, when you keep a promise to yourself, instead of feeling emptiness inside, you'll feel certainty, confidence, and strength.

You've probably heard the saying "The truth shall set you free" and that couldn't be any more applicable than when it comes to being honest with yourself about following through with your exercise plan. Promises that you make to yourself should be handled with care and obedience, as if they were sacred vows. Treat your promises to yourself as you would a promise to your friend, your boss, your spouse, your child, or even your trainer or coach. Approach all self-promises with that concept, and you'll find it gets easier and easier to keep them. Once you succeed in keeping your promises, others probably won't notice any difference in you; however, you will notice the difference on the inside.

Gentle, Positive Pressure

Many people start their programs with vigor yet fail after a couple of weeks because they lose motivation. To keep your drive, you need to maintain positive pressure. If you have taken that first step in deciding that you are ready to make a change in your life, find demanding situations and create something positive from them. On the inside, deep down in there, you want and need pressure. You need it to feel passionate about and energized by life. You won't feel like you've earned your stripes unless, well, you've worked for them.

Society sends mixed messages about stress, which may cause you to run away from demanding and nagging situations. The trick is to learn the difference between bad stress and good stress. Bad stress is frequently caused by taking on other people's problems or becoming agitated over situations you really have no control over anyway. An example of bad stress would be absorbing your boss' stress about a client presentation that she didn't prepare for. Good stress is when you feel challenged and have an opportunity to grow through your hardship. An example of good stress would be feeling overwhelmed about a client presentation due at the end of the day. The stress makes you focused and prepare harder. Good stress is asking you to give 100 percent—your best effort.

If you've been brought up to steer clear of stress in general, you need to rethink it and adjust. Good stress situations help to make you capable and hardy. Pressure is a motivational tactic. Demanding situations motivate you to keep moving forward. During the next few weeks should you at any time start testing yourself and pulling away from the program, know that success will not just be handed over to you. Success is something that you must achieve on your own. Earned success has great potential to lift you out of your depression.

The full-body workout is really a metaphor for life: Have a plan, take it slow, be deliberate, use the correct form, and push yourself. Winston Churchill, who suffered from depression, once said, "Don't consent to the descent." As you keep forcing yourself to push through, your muscles respond and adjust accordingly. Without pushing your muscles to go past the comfort zone, they weaken. This same concept applies to your growth as an individual, to your relationships, to your career, and even to your emotional well-being.

Embrace pressure when it comes your way. Grab it and hold on tight, and you will unleash the best of you. Approach every day with this attitude, and you will exceed your former comfort level (which, in depression, is being in a rut). Positive pressure can provide an influential amount of energy that will help you meet and exceed your expectations and achieve your goals.

Confidence Trumps Perfection

Your confidence level is important at the beginning of a program. After the first two weeks, I hope you feel your confidence growing and that you are not getting caught up in trying to get it all perfect.

The more you believe you can accomplish something, the more likely you will accomplish it. Think about these scenarios: The bases are loaded and the pitcher throws a fastball that the batter slams for a home run. The winning point of the game is a free-throw basket and the player misses it. A quarterback throws to the running back, but an opposing player intercepts the pass. These players might get down on themselves, but if they lose their confidence, they will lose their energy and ultimately their internal drive, or motivation. Instead of playing to win the game, they will play not to lose the game. Maybe not intentionally, but their lack of self-confidence will cause them to do just that.

Successful people, no matter what their profession, reach that success because they had the drive, energy, and talent to make it that far. They groomed and maintained their confidence through the entire route of discovery and achievement. They all operate from a place of conviction and try to perform their best consistently. You may not get every single thing correct, but you will feel confident and strong while maintaining your drive.

Cardio Exercises

As discussed in Chapter 3, you are to do the MMSMR, or strength-training workout, one day per week. Typically, the following day is a day of rest. If you are sore or feel antsy, go ahead and do a moderate to easy walk or bike ride. Listen to your body, and if it wants to keep moving, go ahead, but you don't need to do anything aerobic (high-intensity) on that day. The other five days are flexible. Not only will you be choosing which activities to do, you will be planning the time of day, your clothes, your music or reading materials, and whatever else that will give you the best positioning to execute your plan. Some of the activities include, but are not limited to: brisk walking, jogging, biking, hiking, swimming, tennis, squash, yoga, dancing (or dance class at the gym), rowing, stationary exercise machines (bike, treadmill, elliptical). Let's talk about a few of them.

Brisk Walking

Walking is the most natural form of physical activity for people. You are ideally suited for this type of exercise. In its simplest form, walking is a matter of putting one foot in front of the other—something that you mastered by around one year of age. Walking has become a popular form of exercise because it can be done almost anywhere at any time. Choosing walking as your preferred type of exercise has several additional advantages:

- Requires little time and effort to learn the proper technique (in terms of doing it as a cardio activity)
- Costs little or nothing to get started
- Has a low injury rate
- Allows you to become more and more physically fit, as long as you walk long enough, fast enough, or often enough
- Travels with you anywhere
- Helps prevent osteoporosis

Proper walking technique: To get the most out of your walking program, you need to pay special attention to your form. The most common mistake that walkers make is bending forward too much at the waist. This can lead to problems in your lower back, hips, and neck. While you shouldn't force yourself to be ramrod straight, your posture should be "naturally tall." Try to relax your shoulders, widen your chest, and pull your stomach muscles gently inward. Keep your head and chin up and focus your attention straight ahead. Think in terms of "walking proud" rather than "walking shy."

Most experts believe that it is important to relax your hands, and your arms should swing gently past your hips. At the uppermost position, your hands should be approximately level with your breastbone. On the downswing, your hands should gently brush your hips. And finally, it is important that you learn to "roll." Always try to land on your heels, then roll your feet forward, pushing off with your toes. If you are thinking that all of this sounds pretty complicated, don't despair. Most people walk with pretty good form already. We just need a little fine-tuning from time to time. For this reason, it is always a good idea to take yourself through a head-to-toe checklist every once in a while.

Think safety: If you walk alone, carry identification and your cell phone. It is also important to pay attention to what is going on around you. Don't assume that drivers see you as you approach an intersection. Even if you have the green light, cars that are turning still may not see you, so walk defensively. Avoid deserted routes if possible; it is always safer to walk in a public place. And finally, if you walk at night, remember to wear reflective clothing.

Walk at a good pace: Perhaps a good guideline is to walk as fast as you comfortably can so that you are breathing hard but not out of breath. Don't overdo it in the beginning so that you are struggling too much at the end; but keep in mind that a somewhat faster walking pace will get the brain juices flowing, burn more calories, and give you greater fitness gains.

Sneak in a walk whenever possible: Try leaving your car at home and walk to do your errands. Increase your distance to an entrance by parking your car at the outside perimeter of the parking lot. These little extras add up over time. Recent evidence suggests that "accumulated exercise" during the day really pays off, and it is something you can do for the rest of your life.

Consider using hand weights: Many experts have come to realize the value of hand and leg weights when walking. Just be careful to start with a weight that is not too heavy for you. You want just enough weight to offer a little resistance, as this can speed up the fitness process. You attach these weights to your wrists and ankles with Velcro. They are relatively inexpensive and can be purchased in most department stores.

Enjoy yourself: Do whatever it takes to have fun walking. Remember, the more you enjoy it, the easier it will be to stick with your program.

If you get sore, take some time off: If you find your muscles are really hurting, take the next day off. If you are only moderately sore, walking slowly might actually help to keep the soreness (technically known as lactic acid) circulating and moving out of you. You may also want to consider using an over-the-counter product such as Deep Cold.

What You Need

- Water bottle, even if you have to hold it while walking; drink plenty of water, even before you are thirsty
- Good pair of walking shoes
- Cell phone
- Weather gear for sun, rain, or cold (sunglasses, visor, rain gear, gloves)
- iPod or MP3 player
- Map of route

Jogging

Like walking, jogging is a relatively simple activity that you can do anywhere. You don't need a bagful of equipment, a swimming pool, or a car rack. Jogging is a great exercise for the heart and lungs, and you can feel its benefits fairly quickly. It is not for everybody, however, as it can cause knee, lower back, and other joint pain if you have any mechanical (skeletal) problems. For example, some people have a tilted pelvis, and the pounding of jogging can cause unnecessary lower back strain; for others, one leg is shorter than the other, which can cause hip and low back pain. If you are not built to run, then don't force it. You can experience all of the physical benefits with other exercises on the list.

Proper jogging technique: Jogging and running are interesting activities in that you really can't compare your technique to someone else's. This is because your technique is determined to a large extent by your skeletal-muscular system, which is as unique to you as your DNA. Your height, length of your lower and upper legs, placement of your kneecap, joint flexibility, muscle mass, and weight all factor into how you run. For this reason, you don't need to worry too much about your form, as it is probably already in a groove that suits your body.

You want to relax your shoulders and not clench your arms or hands, as that carries unnecessary tension in other parts of your body. I remember when I was a part of a running club and the coach ran up beside me for a while and said, "That's good, I can't hear your feet as they meet the pavement." Jog tall and proud, don't pound the pavement unnecessarily, look about thirty feet ahead of you, and then down to the ground in front of you as needed.

Walk/jog alternating: You may need to ease into your jogging by starting with a couple minutes of walking followed by a couple of minutes of jogging, in order to get your heart rate up. As you get better and better at jogging, you will want to have one-minute bursts of sprinting at about every four- or five-minute interval, to maintain a good intensity.

Run smoothly: Try not to take too long of strides or bounce while you jog as this may tire you out unnecessarily. Get into a relaxed but challenging pace and enjoy.

Watch out for motorists: If you run on the road, run facing traffic and wear reflective, bright clothing even if it is not dark outside. Follow traffic signals and assume the driver making a turn does not see you, unless you see him or her looking at you and giving you the right of way.

What You Need

- Water bottle, even if you have to hold it during the run; drink plenty of it, even before you are thirsty
- Good pair of running shoes
- Cell phone
- Weather gear for sun, rain, or cold (sunglasses, visor, rain gear, gloves)
- iPod or MP3 player
- Map of route
- Sweat bands or hand towel

Swimming

Mirror, mirror on the wall, what's the fairest exercise of all? Most would agree that swimming takes the cake. It is one of the most complete forms of exercise, has zero-impact on your joints, stretches all your major muscle groups, and, because you are using your whole body, gives you a great aerobic workout.

Proper swimming technique: If you do not feel comfortable enough with your swimming stroke to swim for a twenty-minute period, enroll in a class or recruit a friend who is an experienced swimmer to help you increase your exercise time. The few points that I will go over refer to freestyle swimming, although you can get a good workout from other strokes, as well.

First, use your full reach when stroking, meaning, reach out as far as you can, then pull your arm all the way through the water so that your hand brushes your thigh. Kick using your entire leg; do not kick up and down from your knees. Try not to kick too deeply and don't let your feet break the water's surface.

These pointers will help you get the most power from your stroke and will help you have an efficient workout with less effort.

Consider using aids: Kickboards, fins, and water gloves can all make the workout more enjoyable as you build strength. You will be more buoyant and therefore able to work on your form, as well as move fast enough to get a good workout.

Take a refresher course: Swimming relies on technique more than most other sports, so it may be a good idea to take a refresher lesson or two so that you feel even more efficient and competent.

Planning: Time your swim so that it is not occurring directly after a meal. If you are in open water, be sure someone is nearby who is an experienced swimmer; you never want to swim alone.

Managing boredom: While swimming is an excellent all-around exercise, it doesn't offer the same stimulation as some other activities. When you swim, you're missing sights, sounds, and socializing with others, to name a few. You can find water-proof music devices online, and you may also want to consider other water activities such as water running or water aerobics.

What You Need

- Swim suit
- Goggles (optional)
- Bathing cap (optional)
- Swimming aid, such as a kickboard or fins
- Swimming pool or open water

Bicycling

Most of us learned to ride a bike when we were quite young. Becoming a good cyclist and getting a great workout from your rides, however, may mean putting in some work on your technique. The most often cited advantages of cycling include having no impact on your joints (many cyclists are ex-joggers), being easy to see progress, getting a great workout (cycling at 12 miles per hour burns almost as many calories as jogging), varying your routes, and being a social activity.

Proper cycling technique: Cycling involves body position, gear shifting, and peddling. If even one of these is out of synch, it can throw off your workout and cause injury. Because you are in a crouched position for an extended period of time, it is important to have your bike fitted to your body. Any respectable bike shop should be able to help you with this. Your best body position is to lean slightly forward, so that you are slicing through the head wind with minimal drag. As you cycle, you want to change your hand position frequently to avoid cramping or stiffness during a long ride. There is no need to hold on too tight, just a light tension in your grip suffices. Proper gear shifting helps you ride efficiently and prevents suffering unnecessarily when going up hills. You want to get into a certain rhythm and then shift your gears in order to maintain a steady pace.

Learn how to fix a flat: You never want to be stranded alone, so it is important to have a flat tire kit attached to your bike. Ask the bike shop pro to show you how to use it. Or, sign up for a bike repair class.

Never squeeze your front brakes hard: Flying over the handlebars is not a technique you want to experience. Save the flying for the airlines. Squeeze your brakes gradually and gently.

Follow the rules of the road: Stop at all stop signs, obey all traffic laws, and use hand signals to let drivers know when and where you are turning. If you're not familiar with the hand signals, look them up online or ask someone at the bike shop to explain them. Again, assume the driver of a vehicle doesn't see you. This could actually save your life.

Know your gears: The lower gears (smaller numbers) make it easier for you to pedal and are useful when riding uphill. Use the higher gears (larger numbers) when going downhill or to go faster when riding on flat land. The higher gears force your legs to work harder, so you may have to work up to them. Learn what you and your bike can and cannot do and get used to changing gears on different slopes. Practice your timing before heading up big hills. Down-shifting before getting to the hill reduces the risk of jamming your chain or gears.

Know your limit: Start out biking on fairly flat surfaces, if possible. And if you haven't biked in a while, just go a short distance at first.

Remember that you must have enough energy to make the return trip—don't go so far that you have to walk your bike back home.

What You Need

- Bicycle, preferably with a water bottle rack and pouch
- Water bottle; drink plenty of it, even before you are thirsty
- Bike helmet
- Bike repair kit
- Cell phone
- Map of route
- Weather gear for sun, rain, or cold (sunglasses, visor, rain gear, gloves)

Aerobic Classes

Aerobic dance and step classes provide an excellent full-body workout as well as a social component. Exercise rarely becomes boring when you go to different classes, as the music and instructors add variety. If you cannot find the right class for you, try doing aerobics with a DVD in the privacy of your home. If you have knee or back problems, you may need to tone down your movements to avoid overuse.

Start with the lowest level: If you haven't done an aerobics class before, start with a beginner class. You may want to forego the arm movements and focus on your footwork until you get the hang of it. Everyone else was a beginner at one point, so don't feel shy or embarrassed about not getting it for a while, just have fun and move your body.

Find an instructor you like: You may need to ask around or try a few classes to see which instructors you can easily follow and which ones play the music you like. Be patient with yourself as you go through the inevitable learning curve, and keep in mind that no one learns the moves overnight.

Hydrate: Drink water before, during, and after class.

What You Need

- Proper clothing and shoes
- Water bottle; drink plenty of water, even before you are thirsty
- Sweat bands or hand towel

These cardio exercises have been shown to have the most potential to improve mental health. By following the advice in this chapter, you have the information you need to choose which exercise(s) is best for you. Hopefully, you can vary them and mix them up so they will feel fresh each time you do them.

Exercise Routine: Week Two

Using the strategy tips in Chapter 2, decide what time of day you want to do the MMSMR and which cardio exercises you plan on doing the other five days of the week (typically, the day after strength training is a day of rest). Use Chart 4.6 to map out your week.

Remember, on the day that you do your strength training:

Go for a brisk, ten-minute warm-up walk. Upon your return, find an area in your home or gym, preferably in front of a mirror, to (nonjudgmentally) observe your form.
Do exercise 1 from the MMSMR (page 49).
Do exercise 2 or 3 from the MMSMR (page 50).
Do exercises 4–8 from the MMSMR (page 51).

On the other five days, select a cardio activity and find a time during the day to work out. Consider this an unbreakable appointment you have made with yourself.

Vision of Your Future

Though hope and optimism can keep you going, they will not be strong enough to sustain you over the long haul. Your determination, belief, and confidence are a must. Your outlook should be that of thrill and curiosity. The pride you feel when you see the outcomes of your efforts will be inexplicable.

As time passes, you will get better and better at normalizing exercise, and your journey will become smoother. The future you see will have greater

Chart 4.6	**Week Two**						
	Day 1 Date:	Day 2 Date:	Day 3 Date:	Day 4 Date:	Day 5 Date:	Day 6 Date:	Day 7 Date:
Time of day							
Type of exercise							
Intensity (easy-hard)							
How long?							
Pre-exercise mood							
Post-exercise mood							
Music, TV, other notes							

clarity. Everything you will be doing in these two weeks in terms of exercise are external manifestations of what's happening in your mind and body. Your mind is freer to think things through and go after what you really, truly want. You are starting to enjoy rehearsing your plans in your mind. You are accepting that you have to continue to coach yourself on your goals.

When you were a toddler, your mind generated ideas spontaneously and without self-judgment. It worked unfailingly for you. You probably believed that anything was possible. Uncertainty and impossibilities are things that your mind became programmed to believe. Now you have to view the world as a toddler again. Open yourself up to the notion that you can change.

If things don't fall into place the way you want them to over the next few weeks, keep going. This is your challenge, your gentle pressure. Reread the first chapter, return to your journal. Rise up again and remember that the strength of your positive future vision is much stronger than any worries you may have over an imaginary downfall.

Indulging in activities that will bring you closer to accomplishing your goals will help you feel at peace. It will help you feel strong and confident that in the future, if anything difficult or unexpected comes up, you will be able to handle it using the best of your abilities at the time and continue to become healthier.

Inner Strength

A healthy body is the result of a healthy mind and vice-versa. Depression stagnates potential. Look in the mirror. You have an inner strength, even if you don't realize it. Believe me, you have it. You're surviving depression, and that takes an incredible amount of strength. Day by day we will be tapping into your inner strength to find the resources to fight off delaying your recovery. Your body is the temple of your mind and soul. Losing your vision first appears as an innocent thought: *Oh heck, I just didn't have time today. I'll do it tomorrow.* Catch those thoughts before they turn into a full-blown relapse. Question them, each time, and then take the right action.

Many of the men and women I have worked with have described feeling more confident, empowered, and pumped with self-respect and self-esteem when they stay consistent with their plan for the day. Then they get up and do it all over again—keeping their word to themselves day after day. They tell me that other people seem more drawn to them. Their lives become more successful, professionally and emotionally. They get into relationships, start dating, and their rapport with others improves; they report better sexual intimacy with their significant other. Taking action opens doors that you most likely don't even know exist. Consider Joan's story.

Joan, a forty-three-year-old woman, had never learned to express her problems; she kept them all to herself. She was afraid of confronting the fact that she felt miserable. She realized that the first solution to her problem was in accepting the fact that a problem *did* exist, and that not acknowledging it was not going to help. She felt like she was slowly dying and was trapped in cages that she built around her—cages she would then fill with sadness. She was consumed with negative self-talk and didn't seem to care about herself or anyone around her. And it just got worse and worse. It got out of control. She felt helpless and caught in a labyrinth with no exit.

"Something kept telling me that I am not a failure. Yet I felt ruled by negativity; it was like a shadow that was slowly consuming me. Then I asked myself: *What is the purpose of my life?*" She knew she needed to do something but she felt paralyzed. Her world was crumbling around her.

It was at this point that Joan began to search for answers. She began searching the Web for answers and came across my site for PsychFit. When she came to my office, she felt like she had given up, that she had never been as large or as out of shape.

When she joined the program, she had no clue about what type of diet or exercise regimen she should follow. After a week, she started to notice a change within herself and her thinking. She now had goals, a focus, and a brighter outlook. "Each day, I felt confident and it just kept growing. I could finally move on. I had a motive. Even though I couldn't achieve all the goals I had set, I never quit; I got up every time I fell, to rise even stronger."

This new, positive outlook gave her strength. Every day, she could see a change in her as she worked out. She realized that just spending hours and hours thinking about her problems was a waste of time. And she learned that fretting about lost time kept her in her own little private torture chamber. The program helped her to set her mind free, and she began forgiving herself and others and slowly left the cages she had built for herself. She came to me wanting to look and feel good, but she got more than that.

Joan took a good hard look at all the emotional weight she was carrying around in the form of sadness at her boyfriend for accepting a transfer and moving away, anger at her boss for not promoting her, and anger at her sister for being too critical of her. She worked on detaching from all these circumstances that she ultimately did not have control over, and focused on changing the one thing she could: her relationship with herself.

Before long, she claimed a better social, spiritual, and professional life. She rejoined her book club and other activities that she had let drop. She found a volunteer organization with events that worked with her schedule and started making friends there. She got her resume together and made a goal of sending it to three different employment opportunities per week.

She finished the PsychFit program feeling confident, sure, positive, *and* looking better.

Code Orange: Watch for Negative Thinking

Thoughts can have a powerful effect in terms of influencing mood and can either increase or deplete motivation. Too much cloudy thinking can divert you from your present goal. Exercise helps you to remain in constant awareness of the present moment. It can help you develop a peaceful mind, which can help you meditate as well. Be a good observer of the part of your exercise regimen that gives you pleasure. You will need an extra supply of this, because, at times, negative thoughts will interrupt even the most pleasurable moments of your exercise regimen: *When will this be over? I am tired. When will I get it done?*

If you find these thoughts diverting your mind, try to think of something positive and keep telling yourself that thinking negatively does not help you in any way. Coach yourself through it by substituting the "downer dialogue" with a more positive one: *This sort of distracting negative thinking is not helping me. What else can I daydream about that might be more fun? Let me refocus my efforts and feel myself work through this routine, feel my body's strength.*

You are exercising more regularly now, and you will surely feel tired and exhausted at times. Don't get too concerned about the exertion. Yes, you sweat, your heart pounds, your muscles hurt, but those are just the signs of a good exercise regimen.

Retaining the Positive: Let Your Joy Echo

Your thought process while exercising plays a major role in determining the effectiveness of your exercise regimen. In order to carry on, you need to think positively. Positive thinking is undoubtedly effective in performing well in any scenario. Like other things in life, a school project, for example, or a project at work, you need to push yourself to accomplish it successfully, right? Recall how relieved and happy you feel after accomplishing the task successfully. The primary factor for incorporating a motivational approach to life is to capture and remember the joy you derive from any activity. Embrace that joy and let it sustain you as you work harder on your next assignment.

It is vitally important to enjoy success. Exercise can be hard on some days and can prove to be tiring on most days, so you need to enjoy successful exercise sessions each time you experience one. After each session, while you cool down, take a shower, and change your clothes, enjoy your success by saying aloud something like, "Yes! I did it! It was hard and I was fatigued but I feel really good." "I finally paid attention to my body and it feels excellent." Or "Good for me! I walked, and lifted weights for a full-body workout today." Or "Phew! That was a hard workout and I gave it my best. I am sure I will reap its benefits with time." Or "Though I couldn't keep pace with the routine, I did my best and now I feel much better." Or "Not only am I relaxed, I feel thrilled with my accomplishment."

Echoing is considered to be an effective strategy to keep you motivated and looking ahead to the next exercise session. Echoing is a process whereby you intentionally repeat a particular feeling or memory of an event on a daily basis. It is effective when you are lost daydreaming about your problems. Simply take a moment and recall the success of your exercise session.

Ahem . . . There Will Be Those Days . . .

By keeping close track of all periods of success and making an effort to repeat them, you will be storing the necessary emotional ammunition for those days when you are disappointed by your workout. You are sure to dislike a few of your exercise sessions. Others are simply going to be lousy. There will be times when you have no energy left and your legs feel like lead, your breathing will be off, and you won't be able to redirect your focus to the positives. This is natural.

Nonetheless, no excuses to quit or take a break will be accepted (unless, of course, you are injured), as you will still derive all benefits from your previous sessions and your next exercise session will be better, if not terrific. The very fact that you managed to accomplish it can boost your confidence sky high. You will continue to strengthen your conviction and make exercise an important part of your life.

On the "bad" days, you may opt to take a brisk walk instead of a jog, replace rigorous movements with slower movements, take extra breaks, wrap your forehead with a cool towel, or simply shout out in frustration. Doing something is always better than doing nothing, and remember: You *will* bounce back.

5

Week 3 — Nourishing Your Moving Self

The remaining chapters look at some important information for your recovery. The focus of this chaper is proper nourishment, as you become more active, and how you may be using food to help medicate your depression, which in turn causes other problems (such as feeling out of control with eating, weight gain, sluggishness, and so forth).

Let's do a quick check of your depressive symptoms in order to see what is shifting and what is still problematic. Fill out Chart 5.1 and tally the score at the end and compare it to Chart 1.1 (on page 6) you filled out for Week 1. What are the areas that are still of concern? No need to get overly worried here. We're just at the beginning of the program. You will most likely see some change but not complete healing at this point. Filling out the chart is just a way of measuring progress and identifying where you may still be stuck. You will be checking in again at the beginning of Chapter 7.

Chart 5.1	**Your Feelings**			
During the past week...	**Rarely or none of the time** (<1 day)	**Some** (a little of the time) (1-2 days)	**At least half the time** (3-4 days)	**Just about all the time** (5-7 days)
1. I was bothered by things that usually don't bother me.	0	1	2	3
2. I did not feel like eating; my appetite was poor.	0	1	2	3
3. I could not shake off the blues, even with others' help.	0	1	2	3
4. I felt that I was just as good as other people.	3	2	1	3
5. I had trouble keeping my mind on what I was doing.	0	1	2	0
6. I felt depressed.	0	1	2	3
7. I felt that everything I did was an effort.	0	1	2	3
8. I felt hopeful about the future.	3	2	1	0
9. I thought my life had been a failure.	0	1	2	3
10. I felt fearful.	0	1	2	3
11. My sleep was restless.	0	1	2	3
12. I was happy.	3	2	1	0
13. I talked less than usual.	0	1	2	3
14. I felt lonely.	0	1	2	3
15. People were unfriendly.	0	1	2	3
16. I enjoyed life.	3	2	1	0
17. I had crying spells.	0	1	2	3
18. I felt sad.	0	1	2	3
19. I felt that people disliked me.	0	1	2	3
20. I could not "get going."	0	1	2	3

Scoring: Your score is the sum of all twenty circled numbers. You will be comparing your score from week one to week three to week five. A decreasing score shows that your depression is getting better.

Exercise Routine: Week Three

Using the strategy tips in Chapter 2, decide what time of day you want to do the MMSMR and what cardio exercises you plan on doing the other five days of the week (typically, the day after strength training is a day of rest). Use Chart 5.2 to map out your week.

Remember, on the day that you do your strength training:

Go for a brisk, ten-minute warm-up walk. Upon return, find an area in your home or gym, preferably in front of a mirror, to (nonjudgmentally) observe your form.

Do exercise 1 from the MMSMR (page 49).

Do exercise 2 or 3 from the MMSMR (page 50).

Do exercises 4–8 from the MMSMR (page 51).

On the other five days, select a cardio activity and make sure to take time to stretch before and after it. Stretching helps to prevent injury and release toxins. Consider this an unbreakable appointment you have made with yourself.

Because depression creates symptoms that cause bad feelings—some emotional, some physical—it is only healthy to want to feel better. But some of the things you might reach for to feel better can be the cause of more problems. Turning to food or other substances to blunt sad, guilty, or angry feelings can create weight gain, high cholesterol, addiction, and other health problems that then create a whole new layer of issues to overcome. How strongly can you relate to this?

If you have been caught in the throes of emotional eating, do not despair. It is a very solvable problem, but like any other problem, it takes some work. That is the nature of problems. They require work, and you get stronger as a result. How important is eliminating emotional eating? I truly believe that if you don't get a handle on it you won't be able to reach your mental or physical potential.

Before I talk about some techniques and knowledge that will help you pull out of destructive cycles with food, let's go over some important information about how eating well helps your body during exercise routines.

Chart 5.2	**Week Three**						
	Day 1 Date:	Day 2 Date:	Day 3 Date:	Day 4 Date:	Day 5 Date:	Day 6 Date:	Day 7 Date:
Time of day							
Type of exercise							
Intensity (easy-hard)							
How long?							
Pre-exercise mood							
Post-exercise mood							
Music, TV, other notes							

Eat Like a Pig!

That's right, eat like an animal! They don't count calories; they don't compare themselves to other animals and slink around feeling worse about themselves; they don't get on a scale, feel ashamed, and then go hide in their den for the weekend. Silly, but true. When you look at animals in the wild, you tend to notice a few things: Most are lean, energetic, and fully capable of doing all they need to do on a regular basis without constantly worrying about what they're eating. Without counting carbs or maintaining a strict diet, wild animals do naturally what most people struggle with throughout the developed world—be healthy.

Many of us have gotten away from our basic instincts around food, in part because restaurants and fast-food chains dish out hefty and, in some cases, unhealthy portions. We have been brainwashed into believing that supersized portions are normal. They're not. In addition, the preservatives used in boxed and canned foods take away from our foods' flavor and quality. To feel satisfied and get the nutrients we need, we seem to need more of it.

When comparing the natural food cycle in the wild to modern America, one difference in what and how we eat can be noted right away. Rather than surrounding ourselves with healthy and nutritious foods, such as those found naturally in the wild, we primarily rely upon processed "empty" carbohydrates that may be filling and delicious, yet contain no real benefit to our bodies. This is in direct conflict with the genetic hunter-gatherer programming that we developed from ancestral times, where we had to actively seek out new food sources and consume necessary quantities on a regular basis, storing excess energy as fat during inactive times for later use as necessary. Modern eating habits leave our bodies storing more and more energy as fat for the day we run out of food—a day that never comes for many people.

Striking a Balance

Resistance training is a great way to help develop your body's need for energy without worrying too much about affecting your overall calorie intake. As your body develops more and more muscle, your metabolic rate, or the rate that your body processes energy, increases. This metabolic increase is necessary for your body to fuel your muscles and help develop new, stronger ones for you to use later on. Resistance, or strength training, also has the added benefit over aerobic exercise (still an important part of any daily exercise routine) in that it allows you to shape your body rather than simply lose pounds. A combination of aerobic exercise and strength training tends to deliver quicker, faster, long-term results than one or the other alone.

When deciding what to consume and in what quantities, the important thing to bear in mind at all times is to maintain a healthy balance between proteins (found in meats and many nuts) and carbohydrates (found in various legumes and grains). Carbohydrates act as a base energy supply for much of our body, carrying with them complex sugar strains that can be metabolized and used for bulk energy in the majority of our body's functioning. In order for our metabolism to function to its fullest, however, a proper supply of protein is also required, as protein acts to build (or rebuild) muscle mass and stimulate the production of insulin for sugar breakdown and transport.

Another bonus of focusing more on protein-based foods rather than carbohydrate carriers is the long-term energy potential of protein. Able to maintain your body at peak performance levels throughout the day, protein can actually help keep you at the top of your game from morning to night, avoiding midday spells of fatigue and mood swings, which are common in people with carb-heavy diets. Additionally, a number of studies have proven that the thermal effect (the necessary energy used by your body to digest food) is much higher for protein-rich diets than for carbohydrate-based diets.

The most important thing of all, though, is to find a diet and exercise plan that works for you. Wild animals don't go out of their way for specialized body training and neither do you if you can find something that fits into your daily life. Take the stairs instead of the escalator, for instance, or walk to lunch rather than drive. Find something that you can do on a regular basis. It will get you to your natural weight range, often called your set-point, and you will be able to maintain it without needing to go through a major life-changing overhaul in the process.

It is thought that the human body is genetically predisposed to maintain a certain weight range, which is different for every person and can be different for people of the same height. The human body uses regulatory mechanisms to keep its weight within this natural range, or set point. For example, if you eat more than you need to maintain your weight, your body temperature typically rises and your metabolism speeds up to burn the extra calories. If, on the other hand, you do not eat enough to maintain your weight, your metabolism slows down to conserve the available calories.

When observing how your body shape changes over time as you progress through new eating and lifestyle changes, don't be too shocked about some of the differences that you may see develop. Fat, for instance, typically takes up roughly five times the same amount of space on a body as the same weight of muscle, so you will eventually see some areas shrink as the fat deposits are absorbed into your body. Bear in mind as well that healthy muscle mass is comprised of roughly 70 percent water, so be sure to drink water regularly in order to prevent any unwanted buildups of chemicals and other negative factors within your muscles or other body systems.

Because of the necessity for proteins and carbohydrates in a healthy diet, many people have significant difficulties with handling many "shock diets," such as the Atkins Diet where all carbs are removed from daily consumption. Sudden removal of any dietary source can send many of your body's systems into shock, particularly if your body has recently been under heavy strain due to a carb-heavy diet. Let's face it: The very existence of the diet industry, decade after decade, is the most telling evidence of its ineffectiveness.

Once you understand the food portions outlined by the U.S. Department of Agriculture (see www.choosemyplate.gov), you can simply rely on it as your mental map in much the same way you rely on the mental map of your community in order to get around. Once you learn a new route to work or a new store, you trust that you will retrieve and recall it each time you need to get there, right? The same goes with food. You already know what to eat, although you may need a refresher on portion sizes. Now you just need to trust that you know your body better than the fast-food, diet, and advertising industries. The diet industry, with its "new" or "latest" or "best" ways to eat, only serves to distract you from what you already know. Trust yourself. Trust yourself. Trust yourself.

Keeping a healthy food regimen requires a healthy mood as well, as many people know that the urge to dig into a big tub of ice cream or head to the local fast-food joint is never as strong as when you're depressed, tired, or going through a particularly stressful time. The sugar- and salt-filled, highly addictive foods you consume to make yourself feel better may work in the short-term due to their high levels of processed carbohydrates, but in the long run they have the opposite effect. Fast-food, candies, fries, chips, and all the other goodies (we really should call them baddies from now on, don't you think?) cause your body and mind to lose regularity and balance during digestion, meaning, the more "junk" you eat the worse you are likely to feel a short time later.

On the other hand, foods with high levels of proteins, complex carbs, and fiber provide a long-lasting "feel good" sensation that simply cannot be achieved any other way. The protein/complex carb combo evens out your blood sugar levels, supplies a steadier stream of glucose to your body, and gives your mood the fighting chance it needs to not tank.

Sugar: Run for Your Life!

One of the most difficult tasks for many people in today's world is shifting away from one of the more problematic snack sources available to us: sweets. Sugars and other processed carbohydrates, like many things, can become addicting over time and particularly hard to resist. Don't fool yourself, either, by thinking that "diet" foods with sugar substitutes are any better. They still trick your body into producing insulin when it's not needed and have been proven to significantly increase your risk of diabetes (and all of the excess weight gain and health complications that come along with it) later in life.

Aside from providing your body with a false "high" that stimulates many of your senses (before leading to a crash where you feel down and tired again shortly afterward), consuming excess sugar results in a number of other negative consequences, including but not limited to, inhibiting lean muscle growth as well as the growth of nerve and cell tissues in many areas. While it's true that you do need some sugar to keep your body functioning at peak performance throughout the day, this can easily be achieved through natural means. Instead of giving in and ingesting sugars, look instead toward some natural alternatives that can satisfy your cravings while also giving your body many of the natural vitamins and minerals that it needs to survive. Fruits are a great source of sugar and the best way to curb cravings.

Some of my clients find it helpful to consider sugar as being akin to poison. While this may be a bit extreme for you, it might be helpful while you abstain for a few days to get a sense of what it feels like to function without it.

Chart 5.3 provides a good visual of the Food-Mood Cycle.

A Glitch in Your Reward Center

No one ever says after having ice cream, a glass of wine, or a cigarette, "*Boy, I hope this gets out of control someday. I hope I get trapped into a substance abuse cycle that I can't get out of. And, when that happens, I hope I then berate myself and fall into a tar pit of self-loathing.*" If you suffer from emotional eating, give yourself a break. We both know you did not intend to let things get out of control. And it is powerful. The cravings. The drive to seek the reward. Part of its power lies in the fact that we have trained our brain.

The brain's reward center is located in the midbrain, which is responsible for survival. It is the same basic brain that animals have; but, we evolved and grew our neocortex over the midbrain, which is what makes us human. The midbrain simply executes the program for survival, giving us the ability to eat, breathe, and procreate. In the past decade or so, scientists have

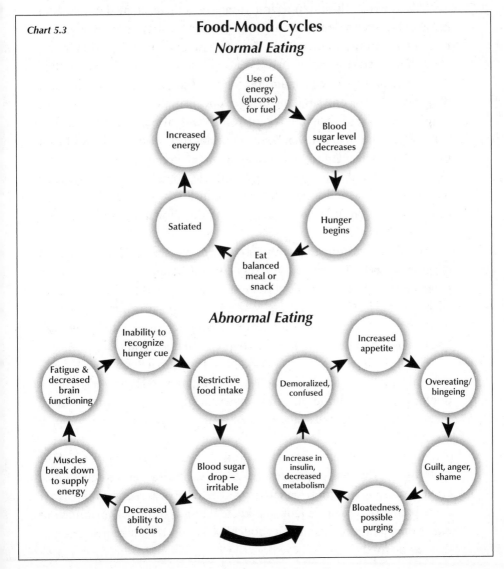

Chart 5.3

Food-Mood Cycles

Normal Eating

- Use of energy (glucose) for fuel
- Blood sugar level decreases
- Hunger begins
- Eat balanced meal or snack
- Satiated
- Increased energy

Abnormal Eating

- Inability to recognize hunger cue
- Restrictive food intake
- Blood sugar drop – irritable
- Decreased ability to focus
- Muscles break down to supply energy
- Fatigue & decreased brain functioning
- Demoralized, confused
- Increase in insulin, decreased metabolism
- Bloatedness, possible purging
- Guilt, anger, shame
- Overeating/ bingeing
- Increased appetite

discovered that there are two areas in the midbrain, the nucleus acumbens and the ventral tegmental regions, that are the seats of addictive behavior.

Suffice it to say that if there is a glitch in those areas, the midbrain really doesn't care. It doesn't have a conscience. It robotically runs the survival program, even if what gets executed could wind up killing you. Think about it. Obesity, type II diabetes, heart disease, alcohol, and drug overdose—these are all killers.

The power of this brain region cannot be underestimated or taken for granted, but it also doesn't mean it gets to run the show and subsequently run you into the ground. Animals don't feel guilty if they have to kill to survive, which is why the midbrain doesn't care if you are miserable after eating the second pint of ice cream and the whole package of Oreos or drinking that bottle of wine and smoking that pack of cigarettes.

If it seems as if there are two of you battling it out, you're right. Two parts of your brain are at war. Your prefrontal cortex (located behind your forehead; responsible for your reasoning, judgment, and logic) gets judo-flipped by the midbrain when the glitch is triggered. It can be activated by depression, stress, and other cues. The brain thinks it needs to fetch you some "baddies" in order to survive, and it does so with its very own cunning, murderous power.

So, we need to come up with a strategy to out-fox the fox. This period of getting out of active addiction is very difficult, because the glitch has been there for a while, and the midbrain wants to preserve it. But it isn't acting out all the time, is it? (If the answer is "yes," meaning you are eating or drinking nonstop all day long until you pass out, then please get professional help. You can return to this page later for relapse prevention and maintenance.)

Getting out of addiction is a quality-of-life choice. If any substance has grabbed you by the ankle and won't let go, preventing you from functioning at a reasonable level, find an expert or support group and get more intensive help. Don't waste any more of your precious time being trapped. It's just not necessary.

A lot of people assume that an addict's real problem is just a lack of motivation. What few people recognize is that motivation is a function of brain signals and that those signals depend on reliable messengers and intact nerve pathways. When we look at addiction as a neurological malfunction rather than as a moral failure, it suddenly takes on the form of something that can be fixed.

What Function Does Food Serve for You?

Refer to Chart 5.4 and check off any of the roles that food serves in your life. What you have checked off creates the internal conflict that keeps you trapped. It also explains why you make progress for a while then let it all go. Your motivation to make the necessary corrections stay front and center until some adverse situation or cue knocks you off your path; you start to feel insecure and hopeless; the midbrain takes the lead and you are back to the old habits. This back and forth has probably been going on for some time. Being conscious of this conflict is the first step in resolving it.

Your midbrain uses these excuses to capsize the earnest, heartfelt intentions that you have when you wake up in the morning. It may not be a conscious thought, but these underlying feelings are the source that keeps the glitch locked in. When you are stressed or in an emotionally touchy spot, it's hard for your prefrontal cortex to stay clear and focused.

An extreme example of feelings trumping rationality is when someone is having a panic attack. The anxiety feeds on itself and gets worse and worse. One trick to get out of that emotionally flooded place is to do a mathematical or logical problem. I recommend counting backward from 3,000 by 3s or reciting the alphabet backward. You can't be in both parts of the brain at the same time—the emotional part (the amygdala) and the logical part (the prefrontal cortex). Focusing on these simple logical puzzles for about twenty minutes will calm down your limbic system.

The same holds true when you are having a craving. As soon as you feel it coming on, do anything you possibly (legally) can to distract yourself for about twenty minutes. Recognition is key. When you recognize any of the excuses that you checked off in Chart 5.4, it's time to execute Plan C^2—Challenge & Correct.

Challenge & Correct

If you are in a pretty active state of emotional grazing, bingeing, or drinking/drugging, here is the first and most important question: Are you able to abstain when in the presence of others? Usually we can hold off due to sheer pride, which reduces the craving; the midbrain, however, is simply lying in wait like the whining animal that it is, right?

For example, you are walking down the street solo and you are approaching the cupcake store and up pops a quiet little thought, *"Tough day, just one won't hurt—as long as I don't eat a big dinner."* And in you

---

Chart 5.4

Roles That Food Serves in Your Life

Check off any that apply:

❏ Numbs my emotions

❏ Helps me deal with anger by stuffing it inside

❏ Gives me time to myself

❏ Suppresses traumatic memories

❏ Helps cope with negative thoughts and feelings

❏ It feels like a reliable friend

❏ Relieves or manages stress

❏ Gives comfort

❏ Acts as an excuse for mistakes or perceived failures

❏ Gives me momentary freedom

❏ Buffers me from relationships

❏ Helps me receive attention from family or friends

❏ Relieves boredom

❏ Prevents me from feeling empty

❏ Life would be too intense without eating what I want

❏ I just love junk food

❏ I want to rebel with food, I've been good all my life

❏ Eating less or correctly would make me feel too deprived

❏ I need the reward of food to be happy

❏ I have too many stressors or frustrations and food helps me manage them by taking the edge off.

❏ Other

Function:_____

_____

go. The midbrain has done its judo-flip and reduced you to being a "kidnap-ee" in your own body, which has just "fetched" its prey in the form of a sugar bomb.

Second scenario: You are walking down the street with your health-conscious colleague and are approaching the cupcake store. What happens? The point of this questioning is that you can do it; you can walk past the temptation. The glitch wants you to feel powerless, because that makes its life easier; it can smoothly and effortlessly run its program of addiction.

The more you repeat the same actions and thoughts (from saying "no" to the binge voice, and "yes" to your healthy voice), the more you encourage the formation of certain neurological pathways in the brain and, subsequently the more fixed the neural circuits in the brain for that activity become. So, by rehearsing the craving for the binge and how you will avoid the binge, you are rewiring your brain to tune in to the avoidance messages.

People have been overcoming patterns of self-defeating behaviors for thousands of years. You are not incompetent, incapable, or genetically doomed. You can take charge of and change your thinking and attitudes and form the basis for healthy, appropriate eating behaviors.

For the next few weeks, it will be enormously useful for you to track your mood and food behaviors. Chart 5.5 is for you to use every time you get off track with your eating. Make copies of it and staple them together in a little notebook to keep handy—in your pocket or purse.

Another helpful and simple exercise is to complete the following sentence: I feel the need to medicate with food because I am feeling _____. (Some choices might be restless, worried, empty, lonely, angry, tired, bored, bitter, stressed, guilty, unworthy, resentful, afraid, anxious, contemptuous, vindictive, confused, exhausted, envious, elated, sorry, shy, undecided, suspicious, paranoid, sad, jealous, shocked, hysterical, puzzled, embarrassed, helpless, aggressive, hurt, alienated, apathetic, traumatized, bereft, hostile, withdrawn, unloved, negative, relieved, cautious, paralyzed, flooded, humiliated.)

Next, name the feeling that is opposite of what you wrote above and write it here: _____.

Isn't this what you are really wanting, needing, craving, thirsting, or yearning for? How are you going to go after what you are really wanting? What will it take for you to have more of that feeling in your life without using food or other substances?

Chart 5.5		Getting Back on Track				
Date	Time of day	Hunger rating (1–4)	Mood/ trigger	Why am I eating now?	Better food choice	Better behavior choice

Finally, come up with a strategy or two to go after this important finding. There are no wrong answers. Just write down the first thing that comes to mind and let your pen take over.

_____

_____

Great job! Let's keep going with other tips to get back on track.

Staying on Guard

The best trick I know of in terms of getting out in front of the midbrain's pouncing tactics is to set your alarm on your cell phone for every hour. If you are at work or with others, put it in vibrator mode. Every hour when you feel the buzz or hear the cue, ask yourself what your plan is for that hour. Just for that hour. That's it.

Since we are talking about food in this chapter, the first question you ask yourself might be, "*Am I hungry?*" If the answer is no, what is your priority for that hour? If the answer is yes, plan your snack or meal accordingly. The next time it goes off ask yourself, "*What is my priority for this hour?*" Make some notes or look at your list from the day before. Most of us can get through an hour.

If a craving starts to surface, counter the thought with a bold statement such as, "*Do I really need that?*" or "*It is being a brat, and I don't play with brats.*" Or "*It can starve, and not only will I not die, I will live and live* proud."

Next, direct your brain to doing something logical, or call a friend, pick up your knitting, or give yourself a manicure. Do something, anything, for about twenty minutes that doesn't involve putting something edible in your mouth.

Finally, focus on the feeling you named earlier—you know, that feeling you want to feel more of in your life and focus on how to attain it without food.

It may take *three weeks* of going it an hour at a time with your plan of challenging the thought, substituting a logical or distracting behavior, and moving on with your day feeling centered and in control little by little.

If you are at a computer, each time the alarm goes off send yourself an e-mail of encouragement or ideas for the next few hours. Your creativity will soar when you free up all that space in your head that was being used up by the question "To eat or not to eat?"

Chart 5.6 is a list of self-coaching affirmations that you can start sending yourself until it becomes more natural. Pick a few that jump out at you and write them in your notebook or on a piece of paper that you can carry with you. Let them be your emotional anchors as you continue to learn to dispute the messages that trigger cravings and lead to overeating.

Correction through Exercise

It might sound obvious to suggest exercise as a way of controlling your eating habits. After all, your weight is the sum of a simple formula—the number of calories you take in minus the number you burn. But it's important to know that the benefits of exercise go well beyond the physical aspect of burning calories.

Exercise isn't necessarily a cure, but it's the only treatment I know of that works from the top down as well as from the bottom up, rewiring the brain to circumvent addictive patterns and curb cravings. Here's why: dopamine (the "feel good" chemical generated by the reward center in your midbrain) produced during exercise plugs into receptors and blunts the cravings. Over time your exercise habits will produce more dopamine receptors and restore balance in the reward system. For someone with a negative body image, shifting the focus from the body to the brain can provide a powerful new sense of motivation.

I hope this gives you further incentive as you work on folding the MMSMR and other chosen activities into your week. It will all come together like a grand symphony with you as the maestro (the smiling, fit maestro).

To summarize, by understanding the neurochemical processes that cause cravings, you can detour self-sabotage. Two parts of the brain compete with one another. The midbrain is basically the same brain that most animals have, and it generates survival impulses that drive the rest of the body to live. You could not breathe or eat without it. It signals your body to get what it demands in order to keep the species alive: oxygen, food, sex, and fluids.

Chart 5.6 # Affirmations

1. I will judge my days not by what I have or haven't eaten, but by the progress I have made and the love that I have given.
2. My life is a gift and I will not risk my vitality by feeling guilty over my body size or what I have eaten.
3. My disorder is a temporarily activated condition in my life.
4. I believe I can be depression-free and flexible in my approach to exercise and eating.
5. I accept my body as imperfect and vulnerable, yet one that I can strengthen and enjoy.
6. I agree to fully participate in life and to sustain the body that keeps me engaged as an active participant.
7. I acknowledge that as I nourish myself with greater awareness and efficiency, the benefits of my well-being will increase.
8. My progress in life is based on learning and exploration, and I agree to experience uncertainty as I make changes in my eating for the better.
9. I admit that I have an assortment of habits that can feel overwhelming and that I may not know how to handle them every time they act up.
10. As one recovering from depression and the habits that entrap me, I accept pain.
11. I understand that eating to cure a pain that cannot be helped by eating will most likely bring more pain.
12. I agree that I may need and want the help of others.
13. I accept that the act of eating well is a positive, sacred symbol of how I am loving and nurturing myself.
14. I listen to my hunger cues and have good foods on hand.
15. Balanced eating takes up some of my time and attention but keeps its place as only one important area in my life.
16. I eat in a way that is varied in response to my hunger, my schedule, my proximity to food, and my feelings.
17. I accept that eating well connects me to all of humanity—that this is a common bond and one that I work toward as I pull away from my seclusion.
18. I recognize that nourishing myself, and not abusing food or substances, is an affirmation of life.
19. Each time I choose to nurture myself with balanced meals and to not abuse food as a substance, I agree somewhere inside to continue life on earth.
20. Treating my body well is a fundamental act of self-love.
21. I enjoy my body by participating in activities like dancing, massage, yoga, swimming, and hiking.
22. I accept that healthy bodies come in a range of weights, shapes, and sizes.
23. I love my strengths and abilities, as well as the areas I am working on.
24. I am not distracted by messages that focus on unrealistic thinness in women or muscularity in men as symbols of success and happiness.
25. I will not rate my success by a number on a scale.
26. I appreciate different achievements in myself and others.
27. I will choose life again, and again, and again.

The midbrain contains neurons, which shoot off a chemical called dopamine; these neurons are located in the ventral tegmental area and the nucleus acumbens. When dopamine is released you feel a range of positive and pleasurable feelings: a rush of excitement (a "high"), relaxed, content, satisfied, happy. Certain kinds of foods trigger this part of your brain to release dopamine. Over time, food becomes intensely linked to one or many of these intense positive feelings. Wanting to feel these positive feelings is healthy—overindulging these feelings through overeating is not.

There is another brain that sits on top of the midbrain—the neocortex ("neo" meaning new). This is the gift of evolution and is what distinguishes you from animals. This new brain allows you to be conscious, to think, to have language, and to solve problems. Your neocortex is "you," and you can override any appetite, even for oxygen or food. (Anyone can stop breathing until unconscious or stop eating until dead.)

For many people, a maladaptive glitch develops, impairing the ability to inhibit the desire to eat. Whether this is a disease, an inherited disposition, a psychological condition, an astrological outcome, or is the outcome resulting from years of pleasurable overeating that have created a hardwired, neurological mapping system in your brain, seems less important than to recognize that there is a pathological relationship between your midbrain and your neocortex. The result is that the midbrain has commandeered the position of authority in deciding when, where, what, and how much to eat.

The good news is that your neocortex is much smarter than your "animal" brain providing you with a lens of intellectual honesty by which you can recognize cravings, view your behaviors, and make a positive choice. When you know you are overindulging, you may feel a range of negative emotions: guilt, shame, disappointment, anger, and despair. These feelings represent the struggle going on between the neocortex and the midbrain.

If the undesirability of overeating is clearly and firmly grounded in your mind, you will use your neocortex, your human brain, your*self*, to override the destructive desires and appetites that you know are at the root of your eating problem. You don't want to let ol' animal brain run the show anymore, do you? I didn't think so. Embrace what you really want, and go for it as if your life depended on it (because it does).

Now let's move on to Chapter 6 where I will shed more light on the neuro-physiological changes occurring in your moving, smiling self.

6

Week Four — Understanding the Changes

You are already at the start of Week Four. Bravo for sticking with it! You have probably already started to notice changes in your body, attitude, and behavior. And this is just the beginning.

So far you and I have spent a lot of time going over physical and mental exercises, but I haven't told you about all the very real and fabulous changes that are going on in your brain as you are doing your workouts. This is an important chapter in terms of building value and confidence. I have been collecting information about exercise as it relates to depression and other mood disorders for more than a decade and am happy to report these exciting findings to you. But first things first. It's Week Four. Make sure to review your exercise plan for the week, to get to your exercise for today (unless it's your day off), and to create your exercise plan.

Exercise Routine: Week Four

Continue using the strategy tips from Chapter 2, decide what time of day you want to do the MMSMR, and what cardio exercises you plan on doing the other five days of the week (typically, the day after strength training is a day of rest).

Remember, on the day that you do your strength training:

Go for a brisk, ten-minute warm-up walk. Upon return, find an area in your home or gym, preferably in front of a mirror, to (nonjudgmentally) observe your form.

Do exercise 1 from the MMSMR (page 49).

Do exercise 2 or 3 from the MMSMR (page 50).

Do exercises 4–8 from the MMSMR (page 51).

On the other five days, select an activity from the previous section and find a time during the day that you will be able to work out. Consider this an unbreakable appointment you have made with yourself.

Take a few moments to complete Chart 6.1.

A Cool Piece of Machinery

Your brain is wired toward health, even if your DNA and environment have presented their own challenges. You will be amazed when you read what a cool piece of machinery that brain of yours really is and how hard it has been working right along with you to heal and get better. It will be impossible not to feel more confident and hopeful after reading about the changes that are occurring for you at a neurological level.

This chapter will help you digest the far-reaching advantages of exercise so that you can recognize and dispute your ambivalent voice moving forward.

Your positive changes will continue, as you stay connected to the value of that change. The research and theories will help you stay in touch with the value and importance of using exercise as an antidote to depression and will help you to continue to make exercise a priority.

Chart 6.1	Day 1 Date:	Day 2 Date:	Day 3 Date:	Day 4 Date:	Day 5 Date:	Day 6 Date:	Day 7 Date:
Week Four (title spanning)							
Time of day							
Type of exercise							
Intensity (easy-hard)							
How long?							
Pre-exercise mood							
Post-exercise mood							
Music, TV, other notes							

Inappropriately Happy

Depression first became recognized as an organic, or biological (and not just a psychological), issue in the mid-twentieth century, when a tuberculosis drug was found to make people "inappropriately happy." It could be said that the first antidepressant was discovered by chance.

Since the 1950s, studies have pointed to the Monoamine hypothesis, which postulates that depression is caused by a deficit of the neurotransmitters norepinephrine, dopamine, and serotonin. But scientists have come to realize this may be only a partial understanding. We do know that depression may be difficult to treat because it has so many different symptoms. And, we know that exercise has a positive impact on all of them.

What Is Stored in the Cells
Can Also Be Released by the Cells

Your emotions and your biology are involved in an interconnected process. Bear with me while I go over an interesting, albeit complicated, theory that suggests that your biography (i.e., your life story) is embedded in your biology, which is manifested as your biochemistry, and, last but not least, exercise positively changes your biochemistry.

Your body manifests the true story of your life and each section of your story can be represented biochemically through the aid of numerous hormones and chemicals produced by your body at any given point in time. Your beliefs, experiences, behaviors, feelings, and exercise are all included in your personal story. These activities are stored in the form of cellular experiences, regardless of whether it is a muscle memory, a neurological memory, or an immunological memory. And those memories can be unwound. It is this unwinding of repressed or stored emotions that results in emotional release. And experts can explain in theory how this happens biochemically—it is called the fundamental chemical components of emotion.

At the basic level, two types of molecules work together to create emotions. They are peptides and peptide receptors. Peptides carry molecular messages to receptor cells. Peptide receptors are similar to your sensory organs such as the eyes, the nose, the fingers, the skin, and the tongue but only at the cellular level. They are present in the cell membrane and act like scanners waiting for the right peptide to bind with it. Once each sector of the brain receives its orders from the concerned peptide, it dispatches a command to the cells' interior, which in turn leads to a chain reaction of diverse biochemical events. Consider a scenario where the cell is an engine that governs all life, the receptors represent the control buttons governing the engine, and a specific peptide is a button that initiates the engine functionality. While the chain reaction may be considered miniscule at the cellular level, it can result in drastic changes in terms of mood, behavior, and physical activity.

Repressed emotions are not just stored in your brain but are present throughout the body. They are stored in the brain via peptides, and the receptor cells store memories. Emotional blockages found in the body in the form of tightness in the shoulders, or nausea, for example, associated with trauma and negative experiences from the past, can be released during your workout. The release is marked by the alleviation of the symptom and is a clear example of how suppressed emotions can be stored in the tissues of your body. When you liberate suppressed emotions through activity, you feel a surge of energy, which is instant and relieving.

Researchers have found numerous possibilities for how emotional release clears emotional pathways. Some believe that exercise increases the release of peptides. So it's not that far off to see how working out may serve as a peptide catalyst, unlocking repressed emotions. Whether scientists ultimately discover that exercise and emotional release are linked because of how certain brain structures work or that specialized biochemicals cause the connection, one thing is for certain: Unleashing repressed emotions can be a life-altering experience.

You may have experienced the phenomenon of feeling weighed down or stressed, which, in turn, drains you of energy. Then, you work out and feel great. We could call the heavy, stressed feeling an energy scar, which gets healed when you release your suppressed emotions, leaving you feeling lighter and freer. Other benefits from the healed scar include the following: Your heartbeat may become regular, you might get rid of your chronic fatigue, and most certainly your unresolved emotions get an instant release. All sorts of stress-related symptoms such as headaches and backaches disappear. Free from emotional baggage, you may find the inner strength to make important life decisions that you knew one day you would have to address.

Emotional release occurs when you indulge in physical activity, especially rhythmic activities such as jogging and weight training; these have a special connection with emotional release. Research has stated that rhythmic activities have soothing effects in the higher thinking area of the brain, called the cortical area. Intense thoughts are known to confuse the mind and typically lead to negative thoughts. Certain kinds of exercises help to reduce the internal chatter of intense thoughts, opening the way for creative thoughts and positive feelings.

It is not just the kind of physical activity you are engaged in. Your state of mind and willingness to be present during the activity makes all the difference. *You need to feel what the exercise is doing to your mind in order to experience relief.* Likewise, the intensity of your workout enhances your emotional release. When you push yourself beyond limits and experience muscle fatigue and even failure, you can bring pent up emotions to the surface.

In the past four weeks, have you gone beyond where you thought you could, straining and stressing and lingering in that pain for even just a minute or two? Have you sometimes transcended into a rarefied state of mind, in which you feel like you can conquer any challenge? If you've ever experienced the phenomenon of "runner's high," it probably came in response to a near maximal effort on your part.

Parts of Your Brain that Work Better through Exercise

Endorphins are stress hormones that calm the brain and relieve muscle pain during intense exercise. It was once thought that endorphins were the explanation for "runner's high," but scientists have found that the endorphins released in the body don't go into the brain. Researchers then thought that endorphins produced directly in the brain might play a part. But it's hard to pinpoint any one cause because the mind-brain-body relationship is so complex. The important conclusion here is that when you exercise you also feel good about yourself, and your whole attitude can improve. Whether this elevated mood comes from your own confidence, the stability of the workout routine, or emotional release, exercise habits can completely alter your risk for depression. People who exercise have been found to show less depression, anger, neuroticism, and be more socially outgoing.

There are four portions of your brain that are important to understand. The amygdala controls your emotions. The hippocampus houses your memory. The prefrontal cortex (located right behind your forehead) controls your reasoning and judgment. The anterior cingula is a major junction that helps transmit information from the prefrontal cortex to the amygdala, located in your limbic system.

The first two are considered an eminent part of the limbic system, which is considered the center of the emotional brain. The amygdala challenges every feeling and perception through its process of critical questioning: Is this something that hurts me or that I fear or loathe? If so, the amygdala reacts instantaneously, telegraphing a five-alarm fire alert to all parts of the brain. The anterior cingulate can also be thought of as the landing between your upper and lower emotional staircase. It is a very important junction and it regulates the limbic system indirectly, interlinking emotional as well as cognitive signals. If it cannot shift the attention from the negative, you cannot even hope to think positively. In order to tackle the core issues, you need to get the prefrontal cortex back online and this can happen when you exercise regularly.

The limbic system is near the brain stem, which is receptive to constant feedback during an exercise routine. The reticular formation is an area present in the brain stem, which is known to receive muscle stimulation and controls the sleep-wake cycle as well as monitors levels of alertness. The reason you feel alert and relieved after an exercise session is because your muscles send instant feedback to your reticular formation.

Because of its close proximity to the brain stem, the limbic system can easily be stimulated during an exercise session. In the hippocampus, aerobic exercise has been identified as the single most important factor for increasing the levels of a neuron-promoting brain chemical, called BDNF (brain-derived neurotrophic factor). This helps protect and grow nerve cells, which helps improve your memory. It is your memory that houses the echoes of that awesome workout you did on Monday, remember? *You want a solid, positive echo effect to lubricate the momentum for your next workout, and exercise is what keeps that growing.*

Strenuous exercise toughens you up, both physiologically and psychologically. It's the reason why we run half marathons, climb mountains, sign up for fitness boot camps, and go on wilderness trips. The euphoric feeling reached during exercise is likely due to the mixture of extremely high levels of endorphins, atrial natriuretic peptides, endocannabinoids, and neurotransmitters pumping through your system. Rather than going into too much science about what each of these terms mean, suffice it to say that they are all produced by various muscles and glands and provide the "juice" to keep your body cranking. It's the brain's way of blocking everything else out so you can push through the pain and go for the gold (or make the kill if you lived in the Paleolithic Period).

Chemicals Released through Exercise
that Improve Brain Functioning

Exercise not only raises the levels of serotonin, dopamine, and norepinephrine, it raises them to a level that matches your interaction with the environment, and this process has been evolving since the time of our ancestors. There are other terms you may want to become familiar with—vascular endothelial growth factor (VEGF), fibroblast growth factor (FGF-2), and insulin-like growth factor (IGF-1)—because they are involved in the enhancement of neurogenesis and neuroplasticity, which keep your brain functioning at the optimal level. Exercise affects all of these and countless other variables in the human brain.

Human Growth Hormone

One study from the University of Bath, in England, found that adding a single spurt of sprinting for thirty seconds—in this case while pedaling on a stationary bike—generated a six-fold increase in human growth hormone, or HGH. It is a hormone produced in the pituitary gland of the brain that is responsible for many of the health benefits we associate with youth. The increase peaked two hours after the sprint.

Atrial Natriuretic Peptide

The muscles of the heart produce atrial natriuretic peptide, or ANP. When the heart's really pumping, ANP travels through the bloodstream and into the brain, where it helps to further moderate the stress response and reduces noise in the brain. It's a part of the body-produced juice that relieves emotional stress and reduces anxiety. Along with pain-blunting endorphins and endocannabinoids, the increase in ANP helps explain why you feel relaxed and calm after a moderate aerobic workout.

Metabolism

If you start walking an hour each day at between 55 and 65 percent of your maximum heart rate, you'll naturally increase the distance you walk in that time period and gradually get in shape. At this level, you're burning fat as fuel, and this begins to gear up your metabolism. When a body carries too much fat, its muscles build up a resistance to IGF-1. A recent study reported that a single session of aerobic activity completely reversed the insulin resistance the next day. The researchers compared muscle biopsies before and after the session, and they also saw that the exercised fibers produced proteins important for fat synthesis. These findings show how even a small amount of movement can create a big effect that you can build on.

Chemicals that Make You Feel Alive

When you place a demand on your body and your muscles sense the need for more fuel, other chemicals show up for the party. Moderate exercise pumps tryptophan into the bloodstream, which is a necessary ingredient for the production of mood-stabilizing serotonin. This level of activity also changes the distribution of norepinephrine and dopamine. When you look at this in an evolutionary context, it makes perfect sense: while tracking their prey, primitive humans needed a lot of patience, optimism, focus, and motivation to keep at it. All these traits are influenced when the neurotransmitters serotonin, dopamine, and norepinephrine are released due to exercise (or in our ancestors' time, running for their lives).

Neurotransmitters

Exercise not only elevates endorphins, it also charges all relevant neurotransmitters targeted by antidepressants. To start with, exercise instantly elevates the norepinephrine neurotransmitter. It awakens the sleeping brain and helps promote positive self-esteem, which is essential for getting rid of depression. Exercise is also known to boost dopamine, which helps improve overall feelings of well-being and shakes up a sluggish system.

Motivation and attention are also directly related to dopamine. Research studies have shown that regular exercise triggers the production of dopamine enzymes, which in turn elevates the dopamine receptors in the reward center of the brain. This gives rise to the feeling of satisfaction as though you have achieved something very precious. When the demand increases, the production of dopamine also increases and this gives rise to clear and stable pathways in the reward center. As you may recall from Chapter 4, this is considered imperative for controlling addictions.

Cortisol

Exercise also elevates serotonin by countering cortisol, a negative stress hormone produced when you are upset about your circumstances (as opposed to adrenalin, which is a positive stress hormone produced when you are excited). This has another important ripple effect: It helps to strengthen cellular connections in the hippocampus and prefrontal cortex to enable a smoother learning process. The conclusion here is that exercise increases serotonin, which helps to control mood swings and keep stress at bay.

When scientists began with the brain-body, cause-and-effect depression research, they felt pretty sure that the problem of depression lay with the neurotransmitters located at the synapses. However, the closer scientists and researchers get to the cause of depression, the more complex it appears.

Brain-Derived Neurotrophic Factor

The neurotrophic factor is a group of small protein-like molecules, used by neurons to communicate with one another, that regulate the growth, differentiation, and survival of certain neurons in the central nervous systems. High levels of cortisol can reduce brain-derived neurotrophic factor (BDNF), but the good news is that exercise and antidepressants work in just the opposite manner. In the early 1990s, it was ascertained that BDNF protects neurons against cortisol in the area that governs moods, as well as in the hippocampus. It helps neurons connect to one another and grow, and is considered essential for neuroplasticity and neurogenesis.

Because scientists can't get into a living human's brain to see what is going on neurochemically, they have turned to rodents to check out this theory. They can't ask a rodent if it's depressed, but they can see how it reacts to inescapable stress. If a rat's feet are shocked, does it attempt to escape or does it freeze? This is the experimental model for learned helplessness, another way of looking at human depression that implies an indifference or inability to take the action necessary to regroup and go forward. If the lab animal gives up, it's considered to be depressed. Exercise boosts BDNF at least as much as antidepressants, and sometimes more, in the rat hippocampus. One study showed that combining exercise with antidepressants spiked BDNF by 250 percent.

In humans, we now know that exercise raises BDNF, at least in the bloodstream, much like antidepressants do. Besides working on the synapse just like serotonin does, BDNF produces larger quantities of neurotrophins and neurotransmitters, slows down destructive cellular activity, emits antioxidants, and provides important proteins for building dendrites and axons.

A Word on Antidepressants

It is interesting to compare the effects of antidepressants with exercise in terms of how they target the brain. Antidepressants seem to start their activity in the brain stem and seep upward into the limbic system until they reach the prefrontal cortex. This might explain why antidepressants relieve the physical effects first—you feel more energetic before you feel less sad. With cognitive behavioral therapy and psychotherapy, you feel better about yourself before you feel better physically. Therapy works from the prefrontal cortex down, to modify your thinking so you can challenge learned helplessness and spring yourself out of the gray vortex.

The beauty of exercise is that it creates a reciprocal loop between your brain, muscles, and bones. From above, in the prefrontal cortex, exercise shifts your self-concept by adjusting all the chemicals I've mentioned, including serotonin, dopamine, norepinephrine, BDNF, VEGF, and so on. From below, every time those muscles contract during exercise, the bones these muscles are attached to send a chemical to your brain which promotes the growth of BDNF. *This is why when you exercise with the intent of working through your depression-generated negative dialogue or the stress/loneliness/anger trifecta of problematic feelings (discussed in Chapter 8), you can make progress quite efficiently and effectively.*

If you think about the mental exercises found in the book while you are exercising, you will capitalize on the effects of what is going on at a neurocellular level. Exercise doesn't selectively influence anything, which is contrary to how antidepressants function. It restructures the chemicals present in the brain to restore normal signaling. After an exercise session your negative thoughts soften and positive constructive thinking moves in because the prefrontal cortex is freed up. At this point, you feel more invigorated, motivated, and interested in your life again.

A Review of the Research

Study after study shows that exercise is a natural antidepressant. In fact, I can't find a single study that shows that exercise has a negative or even zero effect. From studying thousands of individuals to studying microscopic brain cells—from macro to micro—the benefits of exercise in countering depression prove to be supreme.

Research on exercise and depression shows time and time again that using exercise to lift out of your depression is a far better alternative than letting things remain as they are and allowing your depression to burrow.

In a recent study, forty subjects were assigned to either a walk/running program, a weight lifting program or a wait-listed control group (i.e., a non-exercising group). During the study, none of the participants was permitted to take antidepressants or receive treatment for depression. By the end of the study, both exercise-oriented groups were able to significantly reduce their depression as compared to the non-exercise group. In another study, 202 adults were randomly assigned to receive one of the following four treatments: supervised aerobic exercise in a group setting, home-based aerobic exercise, antidepressant medication, or taking an antidepressant-looking placebo pill. Those who exercised at home did exercises identical to those done in a group setting with supervision. At the end of the four-month study, individuals who were engaged in exercise sessions achieved higher rates of improving their depression than those who were administered placebo pills.

Another randomized controlled experiment that analyzed unsupervised exercise and its effects on depression used strength training as the form of exercise. Subjects were randomly put in a supervised strength training group in a research lab for ten weeks or a health education lecture series. At the end of this ten-week period, subjects were given the opportunity to continue their strengthening exercises on their own at either the lab, a health club, or with free weights at home. This twenty-six-month study found that those who did their exercises at home actually exercised more consistently than the other two groups. Additionally, the researcher's overall conclusion was that strength training exercises in an unsupervised setting is safe and feasible and can maintain an antidepressant effect over the long run. Exercising at home can be just as effective in treating depression, and certainly more easily executed, as exercising under guidance. It appears from this data that the subjects seemed to be better about doing their exercises on a more consistent basis at home.

When research started showing that exercise helps to reduce depression, questions were raised as to whether it was indeed exercise or the social support offered when people exercised in groups. A recent study using a walking program isolated this variable and found that exercise, not socializing, results in symptom alleviation. The chosen subjects were placed in one of the following three groups: casual conversation and walking, casual conversation, and controlled groups (those who neither walked nor indulged in casual conversation). The research results clearly showed that those who exercised witnessed a decrease in their depressive tendencies when compared to the other groups.

We know how quickly depression symptoms begin to improve during exercise based on several studies that have checked people's depression levels throughout the study period. One study checked the subjects' depression levels once a week for twelve weeks; another checked levels at the beginning and again at weeks one, five and ten; and a third checked at the beginning and then again at weeks four, eight, and twelve. All of these studies found that the depression levels started to decrease the first week as subjects began exercising and continued to go down gradually throughout the rest of the study.

Randomly controlled trials (*controlled* experiments in which investigators study two or more interventions in groups of individuals who receive them in *random* order) indicate that subjects who exercise regularly over the course of a year experienced a steady dip in stress. A follow-up study lasting twenty-six months revealed that individuals who stopped exercising maintained low stress levels but were not as symptom-free as those who continued to exercise on a regular basis. If you want to heal depression, you need to maintain an exercise regime.

In another recent study, 202 adults were randomly assigned to a supervised exercise group, a home-based exercise program, Zoloft (an antidepressant), or a placebo. The results showed that exercise was equal to Zoloft. In another study eighty-six patients who had been taking an antidepressant medication for at least six weeks without any benefit were randomized to either an exercise group or a control group (no exercise but received health education talks). At ten weeks, researchers found that significantly more people in the exercise group were less depressed than in the control group. Studies that have included follow-up measures suggest that self-esteem is elevated by exercise and may have lasting effects. In one such study, thirty-two depressed women who completed an exercise program maintained self-esteem gains for twelve months.

One of the best examples of exercise's effectiveness in maintaining mental health is a landmark research project from the Human Population Laboratory in Berkeley, California, called the Alameda County Study. Researchers tracked 8,023 people for twenty-six years, surveying them about a number of factors related to lifestyle habits and healthiness starting in 1965. They checked back in with the participants in 1974 and in 1983. Of all the people with no signs of depression in the beginning, those who became inactive over the first nine years were 1.5 times more likely to have depression by 1983 than their active counterparts. Those who were inactive to begin with but increased their level of activity by the first interval were no more likely to be depressed by 1983 than those who were active to begin with. Clearly, changing your exercise habits for the better changes your risk for depression for the better.

Several other sweeping studies have looked at the correlation from slightly different angles, and all of them came to the same conclusion. A massive Dutch study of 19,288 twins and their families, published in 2006, showed that exercisers are less anxious, less depressed, less neurotic, and more socially outgoing. A Finnish cardiovascular risk study, which included questions about exercise and mood, of 3,403 people in 1999 showed that those who exercise at least two to three times a week experience significantly less depression, anger, stress, and "clinical distrust" than those who exercise less or not at all. Another study, from the epidemiology department at Columbia University published in 2003, surveyed 8,098 people and found the same inverse relationship between exercise and depression.

Another landmark study divided 156 subjects into three different groups: an exercise group, those who took Zoloft, and the third group, which used a combination of both. The exercise group was assigned the task of jogging or walking at 80 percent of their natural aerobic capacity, for a thirty-minute session. This was repeated three times per week. All three groups witnessed a significant drop in depression levels and almost half of each group was completely out of depression—in remission.

Although 13 percent of the subjects displayed reduced symptoms from depression, they failed to completely recover. Six months after the study was completed, the exercise group showed that exercise works even better than medications in the treatment of depression.

In Conclusion

To interrupt your depression, you need to awaken your body and mind. This is why exercise is considered such an extraordinary intervention/ treatment method: it helps jumpstart your neural connections, which awakens the mind and synchronizes it with the body. It stimulates the neurons and creates a symphony of reactions that work together to promote aliveness.

Based on everything I've read and seen, the best program is what I've described in Chapters 3 and 4: One day of intensive strength training utilizing every major front/back muscle group, one day of rest, followed by some form of aerobic activity five days per week, beginning with half-hour sessions and working up to forty-five minutes to an hour. When you are feeling really fit (after the eighth week or so) and in the groove, and want to get more out of your cardio workouts, three of those days should be on the longer side, at moderate intensity, and two on the shorter side, at high intensity. In total, I'm talking about committing about six hours per week to your brain. That works out to 4–5 percent of your waking hours. Research consistently shows that the more fit you are, the more resilient your brain becomes and the better it functions, both cognitively and psychologically, to lift you out of your depression.

7

Week Five — Thinking Long-Term

Imagine the past month has felt different to you than the prior months. By paying attention to your thoughts and feelings in a proactive way, you have made strides in many areas.

How are you feeling? Take a moment to flip back over the pages of the charts and exercises you have filled out. Is your body feeling limber, stronger, and more alive? Do you see momentum in the different words you are using and commitments you are keeping? If you are still struggling, please take heart. There is no set pace for your own unique launch. As I've said before, the most important thing is that you nudge along and not give up. You will get your second wind (and third and fourth and fifth).

My patients often say that it feels so bad yet feels so good to work out and work through both tough exercises and tough emotional thought patterns. It feels so good to minimize that habit of breaking agreements with yourself. It feels so good to make your health a priority. It feels so good to see the ripple effect, meaning that as you feel better it spreads and others make more positive shifts as well, without even being conscious of trying. These good feelings outweigh the soreness you may feel when you start working out. The soreness outweighs the defeated, demoralized place you were in when you first began, because now you know change is possible.

Chart 7.1	**Your Feelings**			
During the past week…	Rarely or none of the time (<1 day)	Some (a little of the time) (1-2 days)	At least half the time (3-4 days)	Just about all the time (5-7 days)
1. I was bothered by things that usually don't bother me.	0	1	2	3
2. I did not feel like eating; my appetite was poor.	0	1	2	3
3. I could not shake off the blues, even with others' help.	0	1	2	3
4. I felt that I was just as good as other people.	3	2	1	3
5. I had trouble keeping my mind on what I was doing.	0	1	2	0
6. I felt depressed.	0	1	2	3
7. I felt that everything I did was an effort.	0	1	2	3
8. I felt hopeful about the future.	3	2	1	0
9. I thought my life had been a failure.	0	1	2	3
10. I felt fearful.	0	1	2	3
11. My sleep was restless.	0	1	2	3
12. I was happy.	3	2	1	0
13. I talked less than usual.	0	1	2	3
14. I felt lonely.	0	1	2	3
15. People were unfriendly.	0	1	2	3
16. I enjoyed life.	3	2	1	0
17. I had crying spells.	0	1	2	3
18. I felt sad.	0	1	2	3
19. I felt that people disliked me.	0	1	2	3
20. I could not "get going."	0	1	2	3

Scoring: Your score is the sum of all twenty circled numbers. You will be comparing your score from week one to week three to week five. A decreasing score shows that your depression is getting better.

Take this opportunity to fill out Chart 7.1. It's the same questionnaire that you answered in Chapters 1 (page 6) and 5 (page 84). See how much your score has changed?

Really think about the areas where your depression has decreased, and give yourself a pat on the back. Congratulations! Make note of the areas that are still nagging, keeping in mind that this is a work in progress. If you haven't noticed much change, I suggest asking your physician or a mental health professional to go over the last few weeks with you to see what areas may need more attention (Diet? Sleep? Medication? Social support?).

Now let's strategize your workout plan for the week, and dig into some important material to help you stay on course.

Exercise Routine: Week Five

Continue using the strategy tips in Chapter 2, decide what time of day you want to do the MMSMR and what cardio exercises you plan on doing the other five days of the week (typically, the day after strength training is a day of rest).

Remember, on the day that you do your strength training:

Go for a brisk, ten-minute warm-up walk. Upon return, find an area in your home or gym, preferably in front of a mirror, to (non-judgmentally) observe your form.

Do exercise 1 from the MMSMR (page 49).

Do exercise 2 or 3 from the MMSMR (page 50).

Do exercises 4–8 from the MMSMR (page 51).

On the other five days, select an activity from the previous section and find a time during the day that you will be able to work out. Consider this an unbreakable appointment you have made with yourself.

Take a few moments to complete Chart 7.2.

Chart 7.2	**Week Five**						
	Day 1 Date:	Day 2 Date:	Day 3 Date:	Day 4 Date:	Day 5 Date:	Day 6 Date:	Day 7 Date:
Time of day							
Type of exercise							
Intensity (easy-hard)							
How long?							
Pre-exercise mood							
Post-exercise mood							
Music, TV, other notes							

Reviewing Your Commitment

It's hard to develop new habits, isn't it? Even though you know it's for the best, there is a part of you that pulls for the familiar status quo. You may have had slips and some of those not-so-good feelings over the past few weeks. Remember how you felt when someone broke a commitment with you or criticized you? Well, when you do that with yourself, you register the same feelings of disappointment. Now that we have unraveled some of the knots of your depression, you will simply not want to let yourself down.

Let's talk about preventing broken agreements with yourself in the future. (I'm referring to general agreements, not just those specific to exercise.) There are three ways to deal with not keeping your word with yourself. The first is not to make the commitment to begin with. The second is to follow through with your commitment to yourself. And, the third is to renegotiate the agreement with yourself. These are three interesting and profound options, and each has its place at different times.

Don't Make the Commitment to Begin With

This option might seem like a cop out, but maybe there are some things you shouldn't be committing to. I would argue that putting your mental and physical health first is a priority. When you begin to do this, you may stop making other commitments that you can't keep, and you may stop feeling guilty about saying "no." "No" is a complete sentence. No. No, I won't sit and watch the movie with the kids. No, I won't sleep in another half hour. No, I won't sit at my desk through my lunch hour and eat the cafeteria food.

We make all kinds of unspoken commitments with ourselves without even realizing we have made them. When you truly put yourself first, you make fewer agreements that you might need to break. Your word to yourself and others is more important. It becomes a value that frees you from the prison of your depression. When you realize what it is costing you to break your word to yourself and others, you become more measured about your time and your priorities, and the time it takes to keep your priorities.

To maintain your integrity, say "yes" to yourself first and "no" when you don't think you can keep your word. Err on the side of keeping your word to your mental and physical health at all costs and then let things sort themselves out from there. When you are in touch with these priorities you think twice about making commitments internally that you really don't want or need to make, and you eliminate a huge amount of stress and worry from your life.

Follow through with Your Commitment

The second way to avert negative feelings about your goals is to accomplish them. Finish what you set out to do. That means making your goals reachable. I have talked about this extensively. Marking it off as done—even if it's five minutes of walking up and down the stairs—is better than having nothing to cross off the list for that day. It's great to satisfy the need to keep your own word by giving yourself doable tasks and goals that you can start and finish easily.

Renegotiate the Agreement with Yourself

Think about a friend who has made a commitment to meet you in three days, but between now and then things came up that were beyond your friend's control, and rather than breaking his word, he simply asks you to reschedule the meeting. He wasn't rescheduling due to a better offer or because he just didn't feel like it. He had a genuine conflict and wanted to reschedule. You would, I imagine, oblige the request and live and let live until the newly scheduled date. A renegotiated or rescheduled agreement is not a broken one if it is based on integrity and there are valid reasons for the change.

By rescheduling or renegotiating agreements with yourself, however, you can get on a slippery slope because what you say in the moment, you mean in the moment. But you may not remember what you actually told yourself and you may not actually reschedule it with yourself. Or it lingers as that nagging something, constantly orbiting around your psyche in an oblique sort of way, so that part of you thinks you should be getting to it *all of the time.*

This may have been true about your relationship with exercise several weeks ago: "Tomorrow I will do my boot camp DVD at 6 a.m." When the alarm went off at 5:45: "Ugh, I didn't sleep too well, and I don't want to be too exhausted because I have that staff meeting at 10. I'll get to bed early tonight and start it tomorrow." After three weeks of that nagging voice explaining and re-explaining when you are actually going to start the DVD, you finally decide to put the DVD in the drawer because you can no longer stand the sight of it and what it symbolizes.

If you want to quiet that voice, pick one of the three options I just described: 1) lower your exercise standards (which you may have already done: "So I'm out of shape; big deal."), 2) keep your word by getting up and robotically putting in the DVD and doing it, or 3) rework the deal with yourself by getting up at 6:15 and doing twenty minutes of it.

This keeping-your-word business is serious. Don't let the inevitability of an almost infinite stream of immediately evident things-to-do serve as an excuse to avoid the responsibility you have to get better. Doesn't it seem like there is a part of our fragile psyche that doesn't know the difference between a commitment about exercising for twenty minutes and a commitment about buying a new home? In that fragile zone they're both just commitments—kept or broken.

That less-than-conscious part of you operates in a chronically quasi-disappointed mode because no one—not even you—can be perfect at keeping your word. You can get better at tracking your word consciously (which is what all the written exercises are for), so that you are either keeping the commitment or rescheduling with integrity, and writing down that new appointment with yourself as a binding contract with yourself. In this way, your exercise regimen won't be taking up more psychic energy or attention than it needs to, and you can use that freed-up mental space to grow other parts of your life.

Adhering to Change

I would like to break down the notion of change so that you can see where you are in the process. I have assumed that by buying this book you want to make some changes. Do you know what has prompted your willingness? Usually the degree of discrepancy between what is happening right now and what you value for the future creates a tension that makes you seek a solution. You are in an ongoing self-monitoring process (consciously or unconsciously), and as long as the present reality is within your comfort zone, the need for change doesn't hit your radar.

When a problem takes you out of that zone, however, the change process kicks in. It is when things are sufficiently discrepant from the desired or expected ideal that the desire for change starts to itch. It is a normal stage in the process of change where you don't perceive the need to change at one level, even though things are falling apart and you sort of see that at another level. You might know that you're in a bit of denial. If this is the case and you *do* want to instigate change, you need to get back in touch with your yearning for things to be better, or with how hard things really are in the present. Either direction will help you regroup.

Once you are back in touch with your willingness, you still might not be able to get traction. This is usually due to the combination of having high importance and low confidence. If you find an avenue for change that you believe will work (called general efficacy), and you also believe you can do it (self-efficacy), you will pursue the behavior change. I made the strength-training workout very specific in regard to time, method, and ability so that you would be able to grow in your belief that you can truly do it. If you find yourself struggling with it, rather than shifting to a defensive mode (e.g., using minimization: I'm not really in that bad of a place), hold on to your values and do half or one quarter of the workout.

When you are in a place of high importance and high confidence in your behavior change, there can still be a third dimension that forms a barrier. "I want to, but just not now." Often, in the order of relative priorities, there is something else that you perceive to be more important that is trumping your exercise plan. It could be that making the exercise commitment, even though you know it is good for you, is threatening your freedom (or the perceived freedom of spontaneously wanting to take a nap, which is depression-generated—do you really need the nap?), which makes you assert your liberty (ironic, because it is then the liberty of being a couch potato, right?). This is a common and natural reaction to a threatening loss of choice. The best antidote is to reassure that part of yourself that there will be time for everything and that nothing feels better after an intense workout than the couch cushions under your back.

Humiliation, shame, guilt, and angst are not primary factors that assist in the change process. Constructive behavior happens when you are connected to the value of that change. Your depression has been in conflict with your personal goals (health, success, family happiness, positive self-image, and so forth). You want to be in touch with the value and importance of using exercise as an antidote to depression, and you want to cherish the attainment of your new routine. To do this, you need an accepting, empowering atmosphere that makes it safe for you to explore the possibly painful present in relation to what you want and value.

Live in the present, but keep the future in sight, in a hopeful, competitive way. Shifting into better life habits is always an endurance contest until you are established in the next positive phase of your new behaviors.

The Next Step

I'm going to take the opportunity to remind you here about the importance of focusing on the next step. Place your workout clothes and dumbbells in an easy and accessible location so they are ready when you are. When you wake up, or get home from work, whichever part of the day you pick, your next step is to simply put on your clothes, and the next step after that is to pick out your music; the next step after that may be to pick up the dumbbells. Then, you are already into the routine and there's no turning back.

Internal Tune-Up

This section takes you through questions that will help to clarify and strengthen your conviction. The purpose of this exploration is to discover how your current behavior is inconsistent with or undermines important values and goals for you. Read through these questions every day and jot down whatever comes to mind. You don't need to answer every question. The repetitiveness of the questions is meant to tap into your unconscious process, so just be open to the questions and see what emerges. You don't have to work hard at this, just see what comes up for you each day and take note. When you define your most central values and goals, you can see how the problem of depression is a misfit in your life. The central point here is to explore and develop the seeds of discrepancy between these important goals and values and your current behavior.

Write down the answers on these pages or in your notebook.

Disadvantages of the Status Quo

What worries you about your current situation if it were to remain the same (i.e., not improve)? What makes you think that you need to do something about your situation? What difficulties or hassles have you had in relation to your depression? What is it about your depression that you or other people might see as reasons for concern? In what ways does this concern you? How has this stopped you from doing what you want to do in life? What do you think will help if you don't change anything?

_____

_____

Advantages of Change

How would you like things to be different? What would be the good things about getting a handle on your depression? What would you like your life to be like five years from now? If you could make this change immediately, by magic, how might it be better for you? The fact that you're reading this indicates that at least part of you sees it's time to do something. What are the main reasons you see for making a change? What would be the advantage of making this change?

_____

_____

Optimism about Change

What makes you think that if you did decide to make a change, you could do it? What encourages you that you can change if you want to? What do you think would work for you, if you decide to change? When else in your life have you made a significant change like this? How did you do it? How confident are you that you can make this change? What personal strengths do you have that will help you succeed?

_____

_____

Intention to Change

What are you thinking about your depression at this point? If you are feeling stuck at the moment, what's going to have to change? What do you think you might do? How important is this to you? How much do you want to do this? What would you be willing to try? Of the options you've already tried, which ones fit you the best? What do you want to have happen? What do you intend to do?

_____

_____

Comparing and Reflecting on the Past "You"

What concerns you the most about your depression in the long run? What if you continue as you are now, without changing? What do you imagine could be the worst things that might happen to you? What might be the best results you can imagine if you make the change? If you were completely successful in making the changes you want, how would things be different? Do you remember a time when things were going well for you? What has changed? What were things like before you were depressed? What were you like back then? How were you in your life, and what are the differences between the "you" ten years ago and the "you" today? How has your depression changed you as a person, or stopped you from growing, from moving forward?

_____

_____

Opening up to the Future You

If you do decide to continue to change, what do you hope might be different in the future? How would you like things to turn out for you ten years from now? Suppose you don't make any changes, but just continue as you have been—what do you think your life would be like ten years from now? Given what has happened so far, what do you expect might happen five years from now if you don't make any changes? What values and goals do you hold most dear? What would make your life happy? I know that's a very simple question but just sit with it, and ponder it for a little while, and see what comes up from brainstorming.

_____

_____

Importance versus Confidence

It is important to assess your ambivalence about the importance of and your confidence in your ability to change. These need to be addressed because both are components of the motivation for change. One simple method is to answer a couple direct questions using a scale of 0 to 10, where zero is not at all important and 10 is extremely important.

1. How important would you say it is for you to exercise to feel better?

_____.

2. How confident would you say you are, that if you decided to exercise consistently, you could do it? _____.

This simple exercise is to help you see that there is a difference between the importance of change and your confidence about change. And that these are actually interrelated. If you don't feel it's important, confidence isn't that important either. If you do feel it is important, but you have low confidence, that affects your perceived ability. If you have high confidence, we are good to go. Depression doesn't tend to yield high confidence. Remember, you are a work in progress. You'll get there all in good time.

Lapses in Your Exercise Program

Over time, you will face the reality of lapses in your exercise habits. It may start with a slip, or missing a workout, and then you may suddenly discover that you've gone for a week or two with no organized activity. At that point, it helps to have a getting un-stuck plan. The only goal of this plan is to change the situation enough to make it more likely that you will exercise. Instead of agonizing over your lost motivation or wondering why you are no longer psyched, ask yourself these questions: "Why am I motivated?" "What do I want?" "What can I do—even if it is the teeniest thing—that will counter becoming inert?" Maybe, to be in sync with what your body and soul needs, you really should be spending some time on the floor, relaxing into stretches.

One way to find your motivation is to look in the mirror. Really look. Look deep into your eyes and start a conversation with yourself: "If not now, when?" Put on your workout clothes. Think about the fun music you will listen to. Do some floor stretches as you are deciding. Remember how good you felt when you did the routine the last time. Get a glass of water. Repeat your mantra: Being down *is* the reason to exercise, not a reason to skip it. Remind yourself that getting started is the hardest part but that it will flow from there.

Be a good coach to yourself with the following steps:

1. Understand that slips in motivation are natural
2. Take some time to think about what you can do to make your next exercise session more enjoyable

3. Remind yourself that you are exercising to feel good
4. Try to restart your exercise routine before you start to feel a change in your fitness level

Resolving Ambivalence

Ambivalence, or uncertainty caused by contradictory thoughts and feelings, is a common human experience and a normal stage in the process of change. For many people, ambivalence is the first step toward cementing change. Ambivalence creates a discrepancy between changing and keeping things as they are. As this discrepancy intensifies, the case for change becomes more poignant. Resolving ambivalence is key to change (and peace of mind). Once you resolve it, little else may be required for change to occur.

Remember one of the discussions in Chapter 2? Stack the deck in your favor by setting up an exercise appointment with yourself the night before, so that it will fit the flow of your day and maximize the likelihood that you will do it. Schedule it around the natural breaks of your day or for when it is likely to make you feel best. Plan how to handle the disruption of getting into your outfit and toweling off. Allow an extra five minutes for those things. Keep in mind that going back to exercising when you're feeling fit, regardless of your motivation in the moment, is a much easier process than waiting for stronger motivation to return. Remember to exercise first and feel the motivation to exercise second.

Long-Term Success

Another key to maintaining a strong exercise habit over time is variation. Although you may stay with the exact exercises, the way in which you do them, and the goals that are meaningful to you are likely to change. This program encourages this process; there are ways to add variety to your program to keep it fresh, interesting, and rewarding.

Initially, some of the changes you may want to consider are subtle. For example, substituting music for radio programs or books on tape or changing the music you listen to can renew the fun you experience during exercise. Likewise, changing where you exercise can be a powerful way to make sure that it feels fresh each time you do it. Some ways to do this include trying a new gym, changing your walking route, or inviting along a new exercise partner.

Change Goals

Another important feature of keeping exercise interesting over the long run is allowing your goals to change. At this point, for you, the primary aim for exercise is to achieve relief from depression. Nonetheless, continued exercise possibly leads to other positive changes, including weight loss and changes in the shape of your body. Consequently, attending to and enjoying these changes (by doing a little wardrobe makeover perhaps? Or going out salsa dancing?) are appropriate strategies for longer-term programs of exercise.

However, you want to make sure these goals are appropriate to the timeline of change. For example, it takes quite a few weeks to change body shape. For this reason, you do not want to make changes and body shaping a primary goal. It is just too hard to exercise only for this longer-term outcome. But, if you are exercising because it helps you feel good now, then most definitely enjoy the longer-term changes in your figure.

If you're losing weight with exercise, it is because you have applied the basic equation necessary for weight loss: You are expending more calories than you are taking in. And, it is likely that you have done so in the preferred way—by increasing the number of calories you burn with exercise and by being conscious of what and how much you eat. Also, with regular exercise and the mood benefits it brings, you may be losing weight because you've managed to stop using food as a strategy for coping with feeling down, bored, or lethargic.

A number of body shape changes may be taking place as you exercise, independent of weight change. Certain muscles are getting stronger, and as you continue to enjoy exercise, you may choose different body shape goals. For example, you may want to select exercises to target and shape your back, waist, hips, or thighs.

Other Exercise Resources

When your body begins to respond to exercise and you feel yourself getting in shape, you may want to consider other ways to increase or assess your fitness. These include exercise classes or enjoyable competitive events. Classes can extend the range of activities in which you can comfortably participate. They can also improve your chances of meeting a group of supportive co-exercisers.

For organized events, the key is to participate in those that you find enjoyable. In many cities, there's a wide variety of races available. For example, events for running range from the more casual charity walks or runs (especially around the holidays), to community races and serious competitions. In recent years, access to half marathons, triathlons, and marathons has increased dramatically. For many of the casual participants in these events, the goal is to finish, or finish with a sense of competency, rather than to finish with a certain time in mind. Training for a race can be motivational because there is something specific to practice and strive for on a weekly basis. Entering a race can also provide a sense of group participation, a day of activity in celebration, T-shirts, and other rewards for participating.

If you think any of these opportunities would help you gain more joy from your exercise routine, search the Internet to find clubs for running, swimming, tennis, hiking, skiing, or other sports in your local area. These clubs serve multiple functions, allowing you to participate in a favorite activity, to become better at it, and to enjoy the company of other like-minded exercisers.

Exercise with Intent

Using your exercise time as a period to also work through the negative spin your depression has cast on your life can be a powerful combination. You are using your literal strength to combat an abstract or intangible weakness. With this as your intention, you have a purpose or plan, and you can direct your mind toward positive, corrective thinking. While exercising you have access to all of yourself, the full range of your feelings, and you get to know the real you again—the one you knew before your depression set in. You'll be able to identify and explore some issues that were making you sad or depressed, and you'll start to make emotional progress.

Vigorous physical activity elicits stored emotions. Your body stores, in detail, the times when you were stressed, angry, or afraid. It also stores the physical manifestations at the time—hard breathing or a pounding heart. So when you push yourself to do the weight training or to walk briskly up a hill, and you're breathing hard and your heart is beating fast, you're more likely to recall the events that made you feel the same way at an earlier time in your life. At this magic point, you can work through the events and the emotions, in a stronger or more empowered way.

Emotional release during exercise can also free you from feelings of frustration, confusion, fear, anger, pain, sadness, or loss that seem to come from deep inside your psyche. When this happens, you feel an initial flood of feelings that can be a little unnerving, to say the least. Issues that have long weighed you down ultimately lead you to a mind-expanding, life-enhancing experience, which is all the more reason to look closer at what causes this emotional release, what it might be saying about your life, and how you might embrace this experience, using it to attain insights to work through deep-seated challenges.

I've seen numerous examples of exercise-induced emotional release. Although everyone's experience is unique, one characteristic of the phenomenon is consistent: It is not a conscious decision. The feelings seem to come from somewhere deep inside and take people by surprise. In response, some people laugh, some cry, others get angry. Still others have an "aha!" emotional insight with a resulting flood of thoughts.

So what's really happening here? Exercise somehow accesses suppressed feelings that your body has warehoused for processing at a later time. Be sure to write them down so that you can review them later. The release itself may be enough, or you may want to journal or talk about these feelings with your therapist, or a friend, or the person who is involved in those feelings in some way.

Exercise as a Way of Life

As you continue to exercise, you will find yourself developing habits that support your exercise goals. You may have a variety of workout clothes, for example, or you may have perfected the process of handling sweaty clothes before they make it to the wash. You may find yourself looking forward to the feeling of muscle heaviness or soreness that follows a particularly good exercise session. On trips, you may find that you use your walks or runs to get to know a new city and that asking for a running route or information on nearby gyms becomes a part of your hotel check-in routine. If you find yourself starting a new habit, let yourself enjoy the degree to which you have made an exercise routine part of your life-balancing and mood-regulation efforts. Then go tell your friends about it. Be sure to congratulate yourself on your accomplishments. Your feeling of success will further motivate you to keep exercising. But remember, you don't have to wait for motivation. Go ahead and use exercise to feel good now.

Other Forms of Treatment

Using exercise to help manage depression does not mean you should ignore other treatment options. It should be considered as a complement to psychotherapy and medication, especially if you are currently being treated by one or both. If you currently aren't doing anything but this program for your depression, and you don't achieve the results you seek, a consultation with a mental health provider to consider other forms of treatment is strongly recommended.

Likewise, the use of exercise to mute stress is not a substitute for the use of good problem-solving skills or for a fuller examination of the emotions that arise in reaction to your life. Think about what your body needs and use your body to calm your mind, while also making sure that you use all the resources you can to help with your mood management. This is especially true if your mood plummets to a serious low point, where you have difficulty functioning or have self-injurious or suicidal thoughts. If this is your situation, many people are waiting to help you. Seek their help by going to the nearest emergency room or by calling a suicide prevention hotline.

8

Managing Stress, Loneliness and Anger

The three saboteurs—stress, loneliness, and anger—can greatly contribute to a depression relapse, so it is imperative that you address them early on so you can preserve your hard-earned habits. Having a better understanding of how these conditions can sabotage your program will not make them go away, but it will help you feel much safer inside of yourself, because you will be prepared in a more powerful way to keep them in check.

I encourage you to keep tracking your exercise and strategizing how to fit it into your week. If you prefer to log exercise sessions online instead of on paper, or are interested in logging other health habits, such as sleep or nutrition, you may want to join free services such as www.sparkpeople. com, www.fitlink.com, or www.mapmyrun.com.

Stress

Oh, if only getting in the groove and staying there were that easy. You have a clear plan and feel like you're in the swing of it, as if everything is finally coming together in your life for either the first time or the first time in a long while. You have finally adjusted and your goals are actually in sight.

Not only do you look better as each week passes, but you feel better and you feel as if nothing or no one can stop you from feeling this great.

Then something that you could not have anticipated happens. Something circumstantially unexpected crops up in your day or week and off the road into the ditch you go. Or, something seemingly insignificant triggers a whole series of inner psychic explosions that turns your inner emotional peace into a danger zone. These types of misfortunes happen, and they typically range from an injury that prohibits you from exercising, the loss of your business or job, an illness, a break-up, or some other personal catastrophe.

Misfortune catches all of us at some point in time. It can happen to the best of us—no matter what you've done to make your life the best it can be. But, when misfortune *does* strike, it can bring you down. It may even bring you down to the lowest you have ever been. Your momentum is halted, your self-confidence is shredded, and your mind may spin in circles. You won't be able to make things go your way, as you may have once been able to do.

You can't just snap your fingers and keep bad fortune away from you and your loved ones. And there is no "magic" pill that you can buy to make all of your worries go away. But you can prepare.

One way to prepare yourself for life stress is to expect the best, prepare for the worst, and know that if hardship hits, you will be able to draw from an inner strength you didn't even know you had. If you prepare for the worst, you are better able to accept the circumstances and are ready to deal with them.

An important perspective to keep in mind is that misfortunes are inevitable—because they are necessary for growth. Without them, you aren't challenged and you stay at your same level of consciousness. With them, you evolve as a person. It isn't until things do not go your way that you are fully tested. If you are able to fight your way through hard times you become an inspiration to many. These people are the ones who motivate others. These are the ones who truly make a difference in people's lives.

When you come face-to-face with hardships, you need to ask yourself, "What exactly can I do to create a positive outcome from this negative occurrence? How can this incident work for me in an influential way rather than against me in an unbeneficial way?" By doing this, not only do you increase your inner confidence, but you significantly boost your overall energy. By meeting these challenges face-to-face and making possibilities out of life's obstacles, you are able to move forward in life toward your goals. Plus, you gain strength so that when you face another obstacle down the road, you are able to deal with it successfully.

If you look at hardship in this light, you quickly realize that a calamity is not a barrier but a bridge that takes you on a road to a greater life. When one door closes, another door opens and this is exactly the case with hardships—a new door is opening. Don't shut that door and push everything behind you. Stand up tall, face calamity head-on, and create a positive outcome.

Kinds of Stress

The only sure thing in our world is constant change, and anything (good or bad) that requires the body to spend precious energy adapting is stress. Theoretically everything that makes the slightest impression on you, causing you to process new information, from the touch of a baby's hand, to a car accident, is a stressor. A wedding or winning the lottery can be as stressful, though more pleasurable, than being fired or divorced. It is the emotional filter through which you perceive an event that causes you to label it as good, bad, or indifferent, and the intensity of its impact. The stress itself is not the enemy. In fact, a healthy dose of sensory stimulation is good as it leads to learning and the layering of improved neural (nerve/muscle) connections in the brain and body.

The bad stress, or distress, is an unresolved response that leads to short circuits in the body's normal electrical communication. Distress is caused by inadequate coping mechanisms. Stress is not simply emotional, it is also structural, biochemical, environmental, and behavioral. There is no such thing as a small stressor. All stressors go into one container to assault your body's resources. In other words, stress accumulates, and so it pays to identify and address little, as well as big, life issues. It's almost always a little thing that's the last straw, drawing you into a potential meltdown.

Identifying and addressing seemingly unrelated areas of stress in your life will improve your overall functioning, guaranteed. Fill out Chart 8.1 to identify what is going on for you so that we can start addressing it.

Stress and Your Body

To be alive is to experience stressors. A stressor is some event or occurrence that puts an excessive emotional or physical strain on you. Stress is an internal bodily response marked by heightened levels of physiological and psychological arousal. Its negative mind states are those combining low energy and hypertension. Optimal stress levels, alternatively, occur as the result of activities that raise energetic arousal, reduce tense arousal, or affect those systems simultaneously. And exercise serves to regulate these functions. Exercise has proved to be one of the most effective mood-regulating behaviors, because it simultaneously enhances energy while reducing tension. There is a holistic interaction between your cardiovascular, skeletal, muscular, and cognitive aspects. This implies that change in one system likely affects other systems simultaneously.

The Ripple Effect on Your Body

You are not a machine. You are a mental, emotional, spiritual, as well as a biochemical and physical being. A blow to any of these levels impacts the equilibrium of your whole being. When you experience a symptom or imbalance, an obvious stressor may not necessarily have triggered it. For instance, your back may go out (a structural symptom) not because you lifted a box the wrong way (a structural stressor) but because you had a fight with your friend (an emotional stressor), and your back is your weakest link. You may wake up in the morning feeling great, but in truth

Chart 8.1	Stressor Worksheet						
Daily Stressor	Mon	Tues	Wed	Thurs	Fri	Sat	Sun
Stressor: Body Cue:							
Stressor: Body Cue:							
Stressor: Body Cue:							
Stressor: Body Cue:							
Stressor: Body Cue:							

you may be just one sleepless night, two cups of coffee, and one unexpected shock from falling into the mental, physical, or emotional symptoms of a depression.

A "state" is a mind-body moment and is made up of your thoughts, feelings, and physiology, including your eye movements, breathing pattern, posture, gestures, health, and physical comfort. A state can change instantaneously—as soon as you change any of the variables. Take a moment to imagine yourself in front of a blazing fire, feet up, good music, warm refreshments—ahhh! Now vividly imagine being in the middle of rush hour traffic, horns honking, hands gripping the steering wheel, adrenaline surging as you attempt to change lanes. Notice the difference in your thinking, feeling, and physical being (your state) in the instant that you change your thoughts.

A state is the fusion between your physical body, mental perception, and emotional feeling. It is holistic and complete. Change one component of the state, no matter how little, and the whole state transforms, allowing new possibilities of behavior. Conversely, changing the behavior can change the state. That is how seemingly miraculous shifts in learning and functioning take place with the seemingly simple intervention called exercise.

Flow with it, Baby (and Beware of the Negative Locks)

Being in the state of "flow" while you are exercising should feel like an uninterrupted state in which you lose yourself in the performance, a timeless, pleasure-producing absorption in the experience. When your skills, attention, environment, and will are all in alignment while doing your workout, you are in the flow. It's the perfect combination of your personal skill level increasing at the same time that the challenge of the task seems to increase. If you want to be physically well, mentally well, and productive, as well as emotionally balanced, you must know how to achieve and maintain the balanced, positive state, called flow.

As discussed in Chapter 6, research suggests that memory does not live only in the brain. It lives in every cell of the body. Therefore your natural tendency to learn from a life event can be reduced to a simple formula. An event plus the perception plus an intense emotion equals a brain circuitry that becomes locked in without you even consciously knowing it. Events themselves are neutral. However, when you experience an event,

you filter it through your mental perceptions and color it with your meaning and emotion as part of your innate reaction.

For example, you are walking down the street and a snarling dog
lunges toward you. You perceive danger. Your heart starts pounding and
you experience fear. All the neural circuits firing up at the time of the perception of the danger—the exact position of your body, the muscles that
were being used, the perception of your eyes, and especially the emotions
you felt and your reaction during that event—become fused into a circuit
of cellular memory. It doesn't matter if the dog stopped short and licked
your hand. From that moment on, each time you fire off any part of that
circuit—either using the same muscle sequence or experiencing a similar
emotion—you may fire off the whole sequence of reactions that was part
of your survival response during that first instant you saw the dog lunge,
even if the initial event has long since been forgotten.

You can experience positive locks as well. A happy event, infused with
positive people, a positive life outlook, and confidence can occur daily.
The circuit locks can manifest as emotional patterns, positive or negative,
which may need to be identified and be rewired to allow you to clearly and
sensibly deal with present situations without being unrealistically colored
by your past life experiences. A fitting metaphor is to compare life to a
drawing program on your computer where you can do overlays that you
can lock into place to form a final picture. Change the details or colors of
any of the overlays and you will end up with a different picture.

The Power of Visualizations

Mental perceptions can define physical capabilities. Scientific proof sup-
ports the idea that what you imagine is as real to your brain as what you
have actually experienced. PET scans measuring blood flow, MRIs and
CAT scans measuring chemical composition, and EEGs measuring electrical transmission show virtually the same brain activity for both real and
imagined activity. What does this mean to you?

As far as your brain is concerned, when you visualize an outcome in
detail, either positive or negative, you are creating neural associations that
are stimulated by a real life experience. This explains why stressful issues
provide insight into real life reactions. What comes up as a stressor at this
point in your life could very likely be connected back to an event that you
didn't realize was so impactful at the time. Your cells remember, though,

and so what seems like an innocent stressor may actually get a big reaction that's been held in your body and that can confuse or baffle you.

Managing Stress

Instead of cursing your body for manifesting symptoms of stress, thank it for serving you the best it could for your survival in the moment, and also for giving you a way of knowing what is happening on your insides. In other words, don't kill the messenger. You've had a close look at the container of stress in your life, and the nonserving behaviors that have developed as a result. You have experienced how your body physiologically reacts to stress and understand what this means. Now let's start acting upon these insights. There are three Rs for managing stress—reduce, redirect, and reeducate:

- Reducing distress might mean removing yourself temporarily from the stressor or taking actions that can be completed in a short amount of time.
- Redirecting yourself might mean, as we've already discussed, that you substitute a more positive message that will motivate you to take action.
- Reeducating yourself about your unique stressors is what this book is largely about.

Take a look at everything demanding your time and attention. Does it support your life and long-term goals? Are you having fun? If not, are you sabotaging and depleting yourself? Take a moment to consider some first steps toward lightening your container of stress. Get rid of what you can. Change what you can. Assuming you don't plan to spend the rest of your life running away from the stressors that remain, or manifesting illnesses, you then need to concentrate on the last one, which is reeducating your neurological response to stress through exercise. Without the stress-releasing techniques that you have learned in this book, such as physical exercise, proper nutrition, and rest, the stress hormones will continue to build and lock you further into your depression.

Your body's desire to attain an emotionally buoyant state has long drawn you into an immediate gratification compulsion triggered by perhaps a drink of caffeine, a sugar lift, or a pill of some sort. For example, chocolate contains phenylalanine, which triggers a release of oxytocin, the same "cuddle" neurotransmitter generated when you fall in love or have a child (no wonder so many of us crave chocolate). But these external substances can mimic your feel-good biochemicals, bind to your brain's receptors, and depress your body's ability to manufacture its own positive chemical messengers.

Barring a medical condition, if you want to help your body attain and maintain a state of emotional, physical, and mental well-being, it makes sense for you to do all of the following:

- Moderate the stressors in your life
- Eat right
- Sleep right
- Manage your time
- Exercise

And give your system a chance to naturally manufacture the appropriate biochemicals necessary for a balanced emotional state. The quickest path is to unlock the negative emotional stress response by exercising with intent, which will immediately alter your body's ability to manufacture the positive chemical messengers. Not only can you unlock the hold of stuck stress circuits, but you avoid locking in a stress circuit in the first place. The buildup of your negative container of stress can stop right here and now.

Loneliness

Loneliness is an uncomfortable, possibly painful feeling in which you can experience a strong sense of emptiness and solitude resulting from diminished levels of social relationships. It is a subjective experience, and when viewed constructively, it is actually a mechanism meant to alert you about undesired social deprivation and motivate you to seek social connections.

Much of the early research on mental illness took place in clinical settings and institutions where symptoms were quite severe. At that time, the most common pairing of symptoms was between loneliness and depression. Interestingly, they do have in common a sense of diminished personal control, which leads to learned helplessness. Loneliness can trigger feelings of threat and dread ("I don't like being alone, I should go do something, but then I have fear about the judgment of others"), which can prompt a tendency to be critical of others ("My friends have let me down so much, why bother?"). However, loneliness is a different experience than depression, as it creates a push, a yearning to become affiliated, whereas depression causes a pull to withdraw or isolate. Mechanically speaking, they are in many ways opposites.

Loneliness, like hunger, is a warning to do something to pull out of a potentially dangerous situation. From a survivalist standpoint, being alone makes you more vulnerable to becoming prey. Depression creates apathy and an indifference to survival. In sum, loneliness urges you to move forward and depression holds you back.

Separating Depression from Loneliness

Given the emerging evidence that your emotions are coded within your genes to help you navigate through life, and given that loneliness is a warning feeling that prompts you to co-mingle, what possible adaptive social role could depression serve? I have always seen it as our system giving us a timeout to regroup, reflect, and come up with a better coping strategy. When you view it adaptively, you can more easily move through it. When you view it as pathology, fear and doom set it, furthering a maladaptive reaction.

Let's look at depression through an adaptive, purposeful lens. If there were no mechanism that caused us to step back, to conserve energy, to be a bit more passive or analytical or reflective, our ancestors could have spent a lot of time persisting, flailing, and blundering ahead in social relationships, which could have caused schisms that may have hurt the tribe more than helped. For example, depression can often occur after being rebuffed. Think back to a more primitive time when group alliances meant survival. If someone in the tribe was not adept at social cues, such as trying to attract a mate, joining a hunting party, or forming new rituals, and, after being rejected, didn't back off long enough to figure out how to play it smarter, his continued behavior would be counterproductive and possibly even dangerous.

Sometimes it's important to be assertive and other times it can serve you well to be vulnerable and ask for help. The real pain of depressive feelings might also help others with social cues (e.g., learning to read the sadness in your eyes) in order to help you. That you are in a state of feeling low also shows that you are not a threat to someone who may move toward you to help you.

Studies of primates showed that group conflicts were probably followed by a swift resolution—for better or worse. The co-mingle/fail/withdraw pattern, followed by an attempt/reflect/resume cycle occurred with a less sophisticated brain in a much harsher environment. There was no time to have long spells of passive ambivalence, analysis, or indifference. Over the many thousands of years of our evolution, the simple sequence of attempt/reflect/resume again has gotten quite complicated. Instead of licking your wounds and making the corrections, you can go down the rabbit hole of self-doubt, isolation, and emotional paralysis, each reaction intensifying the effects and the persistence of the other. Our very intelligence may have paradoxically given modern mankind the luxury of locking into the negative-feedback loop of depression.

Part of the process of maturing into adulthood is understanding and regulating unbridled impulsivity and emotions. Depression decreases that control and then makes things worse by fanning other feelings, such as anger and anxiety, which can lead to withdrawal. When you are depressed, others may see you as aloof, insensitive, or even stingy, when what's really going on is that fear is distorting your self-regulation and creating shyness, which leads to isolation. Feelings of loneliness may actually be a sign that you are coming out of your depression.

Your neural wiring does not contain an on-off switch for good and bad feelings such as pleasure and pain. Instead, these sensations come in layers that have become upgraded throughout your personal evolution. But the primitive programs have not been deleted, which creates further complications. Your prefrontal cortex is central to rational planning and the deliberate execution of behavior and is also critically involved in the regulation of emotion. When people are asked to reflect on themselves or on others, the prefrontal cortex is where the heightened activation on brain scans appears. Talk about multitasking.

You need your prefrontal cortex, the executive brain, to filter out extraneous thoughts (negative chatter) and to focus your mind and regulate your primitive responses. And, here again, depression can get in the way by making you too fragile, negative, and self-critical. Depression weaves a

Chart 8.3	**Lifting Out of Loneliness**						
	Mon	Tues	Wed	Thurs	Fri	Sat	Sun
Planned Activity							
Chal- lenge Yourself							

false web that says if there is failure it has to do with "me," and if there's success it has something to do with the situation. The social strategy that forms in the unconsciousness of your depressed mind is high in social avoidance and low in social approach, which then locks in future loneliness and depression. Self-inflicted alienation and little faith in others create the third problem—social rejection. This is one trifecta you want to avoid.

The good news is that exercise helps depression move along; it literally corrects the rewiring process so that it does not get locked in. Chart 8.3 helps you plan activities to counter your loneliness and to challenge yourself. A planned activity, for example, might be taking a Pilates class or attending a local cooking class, and a way of challenging yourself might be to tackle one shelf in your linen closet or to try joining a new meet-up book club group.

Exercise Improves Self-Esteem, which Deters Loneliness

It is common to evaluate yourself in regard to physical attributes, personal characteristics, social identities, and your overall behaviors. Self-esteem refers to your evaluation of or effective reaction to these attributes or characteristics, the value you place on those perceptions, and the degree of satisfaction with what you conclude. Self-esteem is about your capacity to function with adaptability within society, have a good peer group, and feel in control of your life; it reflects your overall sense of life adjustment and well-being. The relationship between exercise and self-esteem is intricate but important.

Physical exercise leads to increased bodily self-concept due to improved physical abilities, which then leads to increased interest in physical exercise, in a repetitive, positive loop. Self-esteem is related to your sense of skill and self-enhancement. As you become more skilled

Chart 8.4

Assessing Your Self-Esteem

1. How I feel about myself depends on the verbal or nonverbal feedback I get from others: ___Always ___Sometimes ___Never

2. When I am criticized, I flog myself for being inept:
    ___Always ___Sometimes ___Never

3. I easily ask for and accept help from others:
    ___Always ___Sometimes ___Never

4. I accept compliments by easily saying, "Thank you":
    ___Always ___Sometimes ___Never

5. When I look in the mirror, my self-critical voice makes a lot of negative noise about my appearance:
    ___Always ___Sometimes ___Never

6. I make time in my schedule for activities that are healthy and make me feel better about my body:
    ___Always ___Sometimes ___Never

7. I am uncomfortable expressing my opinions and feelings with my significant other: ___Always ___Sometimes ___Never

8. I cringe inside when I don't know or understand something:
    ___Always ___Sometimes ___Never

9. In a restaurant, when I receive food that isn't prepared according to my initial request, I say nothing and eat it anyway:
    ___Always ___Sometimes ___Never

10. I believe that I am confident and value myself:
    ___Always ___Sometimes ___Never

11. I openly express my opinions at work:
    ___Always ___Sometimes ___Never

12. I envy others: ___Always ___Sometimes ___Never

13. I believe my life would be better if I were more attractive:
    ___Always ___Sometimes ___Never

14. No matter what I do, I always find something wrong with the
    result: ___Always ___Sometimes ___Never

15. I believe I will never really be happy:
    ___Always ___Sometimes ___Never

Which messages do you want to change to improve your self-esteem?

_____

_____

_____

_____

_____

_____

Write the new thoughts you choose to believe to support your positive
self-esteem, confidence, and happiness:

_____

_____

_____

_____

_____

_____

physically, you notice an increase in self-esteem. As you feel better about your physical skill, your performance skill increases. Other aspects of self-esteem involve a sense of competence, mastery or self-sufficiency, and an increased sense of identity. Internal self-statements may become, for example, "I did it," "I got this, I know how to do this," " I can do this again," "In addition to whatever else I may be, I am a physically active person."

Self-esteem gets shaky when you learned something about yourself at an early age and still believe it as an adult. At an earlier age, when your brain wasn't yet fully developed, you may have heard an off-the-cuff comment and rather than taking it simply as input or feedback, you negatively magnified it and filed it away as a severe, harsh truth. Even though it may not be true, then or now, you still operate as if it is. Fortunately, humans are born with the ability to make conscious choices, an important step in changing how you perceive yourself. I will continue the self-esteem discussion toward the end of the section on anger, as it is tied to that emotion as well.

Anger

Anger is often the result of not getting what you want, getting something you don't want, or the perception that another doesn't care about or respect you. Left unchecked, unresolved anger can become depression. Have you ever avoided confronting a person or situation where you felt treated unfairly, because it would take too much out of you? I have. We all most certainly have. Some situations feel too loaded and scary. But, by not checking out your perception you may inadvertently be participating in a simple misunderstanding. By not sticking up for yourself, you most definitely wind up carrying the anger, sometimes without even knowing it. What you do notice is your waning energy, and then the mini-voice tells you something is wrong with *you*.

You have areas that are touchy or sensitive based on your past, as do I. We all have our buttons. These sensitive areas can cause you to react too strongly or jump to a negative interpretation too quickly, which then sends the other person into an internal landmine made up of his or her own buttons. If you have unresolved anger from the recent or distant past, the following section will help you bring it to the surface so that you can work through it. At this point in the program you should have a sense of your resiliency and stamina, and I hope you are ready to take on some of these emotional balls and chains.

Hidden Anger

You might think that the following list is another depression assessment checklist. However, this is actually a list of habits or tendencies that can indicate hidden anger. Check off any that apply to you.

- ❑ Clenching your jaw
- ❑ Frequent sighing
- ❑ Chronic tardiness
- ❑ Reckless driving
- ❑ Not feeling affectionate toward your significant other
- ❑ Laughing at sadistic or dark humor
- ❑ Not making eye contact with someone
- ❑ Suicidal or homicidal thoughts
- ❑ Panic attacks (nausea, chills, heart palpitations, swooning, sweats)
- ❑ Being overly critical of people, places, or things
- ❑ Frequent accidents
- ❑ Grinding your teeth (especially while sleeping)
- ❑ Smiling while hurting
- ❑ Laughing when talking about hardship
- ❑ Overpoliteness
- ❑ Sarcasm
- ❑ Cynicism
- ❑ Procrastination of things that are asked of you
- ❑ Ulcers
- ❑ Headaches
- ❑ High blood pressure
- ❑ Perpetual stiff neck
- ❑ Chronic irritability over little things
- ❑ Overcontrolled, measured tone of voice
- ❑ Frightening thoughts
- ❑ Violent fantasies
- ❑ Constant cheerfulness
- ❑ Difficulty in sleeping
- ❑ Boredom or apathy toward things you once enjoyed
- ❑ Getting drowsy at inappropriate times
- ❑ Overworking
- ❑ Laughing when nothing amusing is happening
- ❑ Disturbing or frightening dreams

Many of us learned to stuff, or internalize, our feelings at an early age. Does this sound familiar to you? Do you hold onto relationships despite the heavy toll they may take on your well-being? You may have had parents or siblings who played the martyr or who avoided conflict. You may have been punished for saying what you felt or witnessed painful arguments or violent fights that were not resolved. You may have witnessed grudge-holding instead of redemption or forgiveness. If there was no room to express your range of feelings in your home, or directness wasn't modeled for you, it is likely that you have difficulty in knowing what you feel and need. You may feel confused when someone treats you unfairly, rather than feeling confident that you have the right to stick up for yourself. You may have concluded (erroneously) that your feelings aren't really important, or that it's better to not rock the boat. The more you ignore your valid feelings, the more likely they become layers and layers of psychic sludge, the prime breeding substance for depression.

Understanding and naming your anger-related feelings can be difficult and tricky. You may sometimes mask your feelings, and your emotions may shift quickly without you knowing why. Riding this emotional roller coaster can keep you in a constant state of reactivity. Not only can this be exhausting, but you can lose confidence in your own stability, which only exacerbates your spiraling depression.

When you find yourself depressed and don't know why, think back over the previous day or so to uncover something that may have angered you that you automatically stuffed. Right now, as practice, put your peaceful, easygoing persona aside. Imagine you are the most unreasonably tough person on this planet. Review the last twenty-four hours and look for something that would have made this person angry.

What do you think it could be? _____

_____

Why didn't you get angry?_____

_____

Now go back over the "Hidden Anger" checklist on page 149. Did you experience any of these feelings or symptoms? Chances are the situation did hit your radar, but you just didn't know it. Try to relive it and write down some of your internal anger signals: _____

_____

Owning Your Anger

Other people will step on your toes or worse (much worse), and while the other person might be out of line, the anger is *yours*, all yours. You cannot make that person responsible for your feelings no matter how much of a jerk he or she may truly be. Blaming won't help you work through your feelings, and there is nothing the other person can do that will help either, unless it is in a response to something you do. Accepting your anger as your own will make your life easier in the long run, because then you can control the outcome of your feelings. Feelings are just there in the same way your skin, muscles, and bones are.

Responding to Your Anger

First—always—the first thing to do is hit the pause button. Well, not literally. You don't want to hit anything. Breathe. Breathe some more. Give yourself some time to regroup without stuffing or avoiding or clenching or eating or drinking or flailing. Anger is simply a cue that you need to do something. But you don't need to do it right away. It may have been something that happened, or something that didn't happen, but, either way, you want to be assertive in a way that also promotes integrity; therefore, you might want to wait until you can come from a wiser place inside of yourself before you voice (or write) your response.

Second, name and own your feelings and then choose when, where, and how you will express them. When you get better at this you may want to handle it in the moment by simply saying, "When you do that, I feel (upset, angry, frustrated, peeved, hurt, disappointed and so forth)

_____."

You will find that as you take better and better care of your emotional health you won't want to carry around toxic feelings, and by taking care of the wrongdoing in the moment, you put the feelings back where they belong.

Stuffed Feelings that Can Come Out as Anger

Many feelings can contribute to anger. If you don't discuss and work through these feelings with the other person, with a therapist, in a journal, or with a good friend, they can percolate just below the surface. At the slightest offense, you blow up. Then you look like a hot head when you are actually a kind person who just hasn't gotten the hang of taking care of yourself well enough yet.

Let's get familiar with some of these feelings and scenarios so that you can recognize them sooner rather than later and be proactive when they come along (which they most definitely will).

Feeling ridiculed or put down (embarrassed)
Wanting others to do what you want (controlling or out of control)
Feeling like you have disappointed others (guilty)
Thinking someone is choosing someone else over you (rejected)
Feeling confused and unsure of yourself (insecure)
Feeling choked up, sad, tearful (hurt)
Feeling laughed at or insulted (humiliated)
Feeling unheard (ignored)
Afraid of losing someone (fearful)
Feeling low self-worth, that you are not good enough (inadequate)
Feeling unsupported or like people aren't there for you (isolated)

These are all scenarios that can lead to anger if they are left to multiply and divide in their own petri dish in your brain. And you know what forms when that petri dish runneth over, don't you? Yes, that miserable old psychic sludge that breeds depression.

Why do we deny our anger? Because anger can cause problems, can't it? No one wants to look out of control or mean or crazy. It can be easier to deny it, to not ruffle anyone's feathers, and most especially to not have a confrontation. Have you ever met anyone who really looks forward to a confrontation that has the potential for spinning out of control where he or she may be called a name or two at the end of the carnage? Me neither. If you grew up in a chaotic home, then you feel safer not going there. If it doesn't get acknowledged, it will just go away, right? Eventually you can become unaware of it all together.

This is where you enter the danger zone, however, because repressed anger only leads to resentment and depression. It doesn't vaporize into thin air. It causes problems in relationships because when you deny your anger, you are not being honest with yourself, and you are not being authentic with others, either. And who trusts someone who isn't truthful? You may be fearful of alienating others, but what you are really doing is undermining the relationship, and you will destroy the relationship with your avoidance, which, until this moment, you were probably seeing as kindness (the ol' peacekeeper spin).

What are the situations where or when it is most difficult to admit you're angry and then express it? _____

_____

What about times when you were able to express it comfortably? _____

_____

_____

What is the difference between the two?_____

_____

What about situations when your behavior shows that you are angry but you don't deal with it?_____

_____

Is a pattern beginning to surface? It's sometimes easier to be angry at strangers when it is obviously justified (being cut off by another driver), than owning your anger when your boss grants your coworker time off during an especially busy week, increasing your already heavy workload (and you won't be getting any paid overtime). Examples of patterns might include: always feeling nervous after a meeting with a supervisor; usually feeling depleted when it's time to pick up the kids from the bus stop; feeling aggravated when it comes time to start dinner; feeling standoffish when your partner walks in the door.

Chart 8.4 will help you track your feelings for the next week. Each day during the next week, check off the feelings you've had that day and jot down the time of the day. At the end of the week review the chart and try to remember the details of the incidents.

Chart 8.4	Tracking Your Feelings						
Feeling	**Mon**	**Tues**	**Wed**	**Thurs**	**Fri**	**Sat**	**Sun**
Vulnerable							
Sad							
Pressured							
Challenged							
Ambivalent							
Hurt							
Caring							
Angry							
Jealous							
Cynical							
Aggressive							
Peeved							
Cheery							
Pleased							
Content							
Irritated							
Out of control							
Contemptuous							
Hopeful							
Cross							
Motivated							
Upset							
Enraged							
Exuberant							
Rejected							
Depressed							
Offended							
Guilty							
Anxious							
Defeated							
Open							
Threatened							
Bitter							
Confused							
Hopeless							
Driven							

What are the three most checked feelings for the week? _____

_____

_____

Which days and at what time(s) of the day were you having the most feelings?

_____

_____

What were the events surrounding these times? _____

_____

_____

Continue to notice patterns. By understanding your feelings and what is causing them, you are making huge strides in knowing how to problem-solve. By naming your feelings you will have a vocabulary to use to clearly state your issues and needs. A most effective way to communicate your concerns is simply using the "When you _____, I feel _____" model. For example, "When you tell me you will be home at 5 and you then get home at 6, I feel really, really, upset because I am counting on that time to get in my workout."

You also might be noticing the sequence effect. Taking the above example, you might notice that when your partner comes home late, you are far more irritated with the kids than warranted, which causes you to become sulky and to feel guilty. Everyone feels anger, but not everyone experiences it the same way or to the same degree. People often assume because they feel anger intensely that everyone else does, too. But, this is just not the case. Some people insist they never feel anger, but they are suppressing it; others feel it considerably and learn to express it constructively; still others are consumed by an internal inferno that hurts them and those around them.

Read the following statements and rate each one based on this scale: 0 (extremely unlikely), 1 (unlikely), 2 (possible), 3 (likely), 4 (very likely):

1. I sometimes feel like I get a raw deal in life. 0 1 2 3 4
2. If someone doesn't ask me to do something within a certain timeframe, I put it off or don't do it at all. 0 1 2 3 4
3. I easily get ticked off at people. 0 1 2 3 4
4. When I am angered, I say mean and threatening things. 0 1 2 3 4
5. I can get so mad that I throw, kick, or hit things. 0 1 2 3 4
6. I can get really enraged where I am capable of hitting or kicking someone. 0 1 2 3 4

To score this, add the circled number. If you score lower than five, you express your anger constructively. If it is between five and nine, you have issues communicating your anger constructively. If you scored ten or higher, you can become abusive; you may benefit from therapy or an anger-management program.

Anger is not just a feeling that you think about and then talk through. It can be experienced and expressed through three modes: physiological (your body's reaction), behavioral (your actions), and mental (your thoughts). There are many triggers that we all experience at one time or another that can cause upset. Which of these tends to get under your skin? Check off any that apply.

❑ Unfair treatment
❑ Powerlessness
❑ Offense to my morals or standards
❑ Unfair treatment to loved ones
❑ Someone else's incompetence
❑ Disrespectful treatment
❑ Stress
❑ Unfair treatment of an innocent person or animal
❑ Unmet expectations
❑ Unfair criticism

❑ Fair criticism
❑ Blocked plans or goals
❑ Being stalked or harassed
❑ Fatigue
❑ Being let down by someone
❑ My own flaws
❑ Property damage
❑ Being violated
❑ Waiting in line
❑ Traffic
❑ Inability to control an outcome

Knowing your own way of dealing with anger can help you choose the best way to respond. When you are angry which one(s) of the following do you do? Check off any that apply.

❑ Talk to a friend
❑ Blame it on someone
❑ Get a headache
❑ Apologize to smooth it over even though you've done nothing wrong

❑ Try to act as if nothing has happened
❑ Take it out on others
❑ Keep it stuffed inside
❑ Get nervous or nauseated
❑ Become weak or depressed

Based on what you've selected, you may see that you are an anger-in or anger-out type of person. It's usually worth striving to be somewhere in the middle. Finding your center and then discussing your experience (when you . . . , I feel . . .) will help you feel in control and be more effective in your relationships.

Self-Worth

If you have good self-esteem, you seldom consent to allowing anyone to make you feel bad about yourself. Self-worth is the degree to which you value yourself as a human being. The lower it is the more you may allow others to affect your mood and sense of self. You may give others too much power to shift how you feel about yourself from positive to negative. Are you a good person or not? Have you done anything so horribly wrong that you deserve some of the ways you are treated by others? Yes, you are a good person. Hold onto that fact. Make it become your coat of armor. When you feel sensitive to another's negativity, don't absorb it, let it bounce off. Remind yourself, "I am a good person, even if this person has made up a story about me based on their assumptions or inadequate information because it serves them better to see me as less than them. They are making me feel small or bad so that they can feel better. I do not agree and will not give them that much power over me."

If you do not have this inner dialogue in place, you are at the mercy of others: If they are nice to you, you are happy; and if they are mean to you, you are upset or miserable. The lower your self-esteem the more easily angered you can become and the more inappropriately you may handle anger. If you hold your anger and become passive-aggressive or lash out, you are becoming part of the problem. The other party will point this out, which only further erodes your moral.

There is a wonderful Native American saying: Don't be where the arrow lands. Think about how you might be positioning yourself for depression (the arrow) and continue to proactively strategize so that you are not in the arrow's path. Keep your poise, have a grounded posture based on the firm fact that you are a good person and your life matters. Your presence on this planet has already affected the lives of others in positive ways, so don't let someone else place their issues onto you and damage your positive feelings about yourself.

Perhaps your childhood did not prop up your ego enough. You may not have been given enough of the positive mirroring you needed because of distracted parents (benign neglect) or hypercritical parents or siblings (emotional abuse). Physical and sexual abuse also creates serious emotional scarring that you now get to heal through your own self-love. Do you have a photo of yourself when you were younger? Put it in a frame and see what a lovely, innocent child you were. Let your heart love him or her. Every time you see the picture, say something positive to the little peanut: "I love you," or "You are such a cutie," or "You are such a smart, brave little girl." List your own nurturing message here: _____

_____

_____

Call some of your friends together to have some fun with an exercise that will help all of you. It's called "Tag, you're it. You are the best." Ask each friend what it is he or she likes about you. Yes, this is an awkward one. But if you are all participating it can be quite touching. Take turns giving each other genuine compliments. The person next to you takes notes for you so that you can simply listen and take it in, and then gives you the notes to keep by your bedside so that you can review them at night and in the morning. The information exchanged during this exercise is one of the best gifts—perhaps ever—that you will give to and receive from your friends.

9

Exercise, Spirituality and the Great Outdoors

There is a nearby trail that I hike with my dogs that just calls to me. When I connect to the sounds of the bubbling creek, the different textures of the craggy rocks and sandy banks, the visual contrasts between the towering trees and the spindly weaving path, the rocky peaks leading to flat trails slicing through bamboo, it just pulls me in. It is like a vortex of positive energy and it doesn't matter if the weather is humid and sunny or cold and snowy, the trail never disappoints. Always there, nature is. This chapter is about leaving your depression behind, going out and finding your trail, and as you are on your trail, finding your heart again.

Whether you are going for a walk, running, biking, kayaking, or hiking, you get to enjoy the gift of connecting to your surroundings. There is nothing quite like being in closer harmony with nature, and enjoying the communion of all your senses: the smell of the grass, the sight of the clouds, the feel of the air on your skin, the sound of the leaves in the breeze. Developing a transformative relationship with nature, allowing it to hold you in its abstract power of birth, rebirth, and growth, is incredibly healing. Early Celts used to say that in nature "thin places" exist, meaning the place where the wall between you and your God or creator becomes more porous, more permeable.

It's hard to describe, but seasoned hikers know it—all of a sudden as you walk along, the tree leaves become brighter, or a ray of sun profoundly pierces through the clouds and fauna to grace the trail before you, time slows, and the quietude gets a little volume to it. I was once running on a trail next to the canal where I live in Washington, D.C. On one side is an embankment that goes into thick brush and just beyond that is the Potomac River. As I was running along, just loving the day, a deer jumped out from the brush and practically crashed into me. Needless to say, I was delighted to be so met by nature four miles from the White House.

In Chapter 3, I described different types of aerobic activities, many of which take you outside. To find a local club, you could try these Web sites: www.meetup.com and www.thingstodo.com. Each one allows you to browse through different activities based on your zip code, or you can do a search for various clubs or adventures. For other outdoor activities you may want to browse the Internet for organizations to join.

Finding Your Trail, Finding Your Heart

As you have come to understand, your depression allows negative emotions to build on each other, exponentially increasing in strength, until you are at a point of depletion. Just as this can occur in a negative direction, it can also be consciously corrected through your choice of upbeat, positive thoughts. You can practice positive thoughts that produce uplifting emotions that build on each other, developing more and more powerful love and compassion until these feelings appear limitless in your mind.

I invite you to read through the next several sections and take notes on which statements resonate with you. They may be ones you feel you need to focus on or ones that make you feel understood. As you are connecting to the power of nature and are in the rhythm of your outdoor activity, reflect on the one or two statements that feel like a priority for you to work through or embrace. Feel the strength found in your body and in nature that is supporting you as you attend to this important emotional, existential practice.

What to Strive For

Read the following statements and see how close they fit to how you feel at present:

I am living a life that is close to what I've always imagined for myself.
I mostly feel as though I can act on my preferences and that they match my intuition.
I am aware of my commitments and feel free to say "no" when needed.
I can take in my friend or partner's feelings and behavior as information without having to fix the situation.
I feel secure in keeping my private matters private without feeling like I am being dishonest.
I feel clear about my standards and allow for flexibility as appropriate.
I can be both optimistic and engaged in personal change and growth.

If these statements feel comfortable to you, then keep working your program. If not, the following questions may help you clear up both the present and the type of future you want:

Where am I in my life right now?
What is changing about my life?
What do I desire?
Whom do I care about?
What hurts?
What is making me happy?
What do I fear?
What am I willing to lose?
Is there someone or something that is depleting me?
What boundaries can I set to protect my energy?
How do the people who inspire me set boundaries? (What do they say? What don't they say? When do they say it?)

What you believe is most essential to living a happy and meaningful life will become your own personal mission statement. You will want to keep special watch over not becoming so busy and engrossed in the small tasks of your life that you find it difficult to step back and ask yourself what matters the most to you. You may go through periods where you haven't thought much about such issues and lose sight of your personal answers. You will know this when the old feelings creep back in where you feel like you have a chronic lack of direction in life, or it becomes difficult to tell if you are making progress or simply treading water. If you want to have a genuinely happy life, it's important to think about what brings you joy and meaning throughout your life. The more you consider what is most essential, the better your experiences can help you discover deeper answers.

Here are a few meditations for you to think about while walking, running, biking, kayaking, whatever the activity:

Just Keep Moving

Fill me with boldness to follow my heart, to be creative in my journey and to hear your supportive voice as a constant. Help me to continue to make important changes in my life.

Be My Own Hero

Help me to make new friends, find a new love, and stay connected to my positive energy. Remove any thoughts or mindset of negativity in my life. Help me to continue to focus on what brings me joy and happiness.

No Trespassing

Help me guard against or let go of any worry or fearful thoughts. Replace my anxiety with peace and certainty. Let me remember the times I have found boldness to overcome insecurities.

Permission to Live? Granted!

Being more "alive" is simply being more myself. I can trust and express my thoughts and observations. I simply assume that I am worth being loved. By not allowing myself to be dominated by self-consciousness I feel more powerful and more alive.

Unhooking from Fear

I don't let negative self-doubts become facts or allow myself to hide behind shyness or self-consciousness. To overcome this, I ask myself: What is the worst thing that could happen if I decide to reveal and express my riskier emotions that I keep hidden under this cloak of self-consciousness and fear?

Testing the Waters

Learning to be less inhibited and more expressive and passionate than I have been previously involves the chance of being foolish—but that's not necessarily a bad thing, right? I am simply getting used to taking risks one step at a time.

Cultivating Friendships

Friendship creates the experience of being kindred spirits and is, in fact, one of the strongest ties I can make. It is the antidote to the human dilemma that I face—loneliness. I am looking for friendships where I know the other person cares about me—I am liked, even cherished, for who I am and what I contribute to the other person. There is a sense of goodwill and fidelity toward each other—I trust that the other person has my best interests at heart and is a loyal ally, just as I am for him or her.

Responsible Reactivity

I can be changed by what happens to me, but I refuse to be reduced by it. I don't need to go into defense mode. Being right is a dead-end. It's all I get. I don't get to solve the problem, reduce the conflict, or even stop feeling angry. And I definitely don't get to feel closer to the person. I can be open and still feel safe.

Embracing What is Difficult

Every unhappy experience allows me to obtain greater understanding about myself, until I learn to avoid those experiences. Those difficult people in my life are really just teachers. All are calculated to bring me to higher levels of knowledge.

Mindfulness, Relaxation and Corrective Thinking

The following will help you on a daily basis as you develop a proactive positive milieu in your mind:

- Practice being alert, fully present, and attentive by taking in the colors, sounds, smells and sights around you in a deliberate, retentive way.
- Befriend yourself by letting go of self-criticism.
- Remember that you have the ability to make peace with yourself right now, in this very moment, regardless of what else is going on around you. Cultivate gratitude, appreciation, optimism, and kindness. Let it grow inside you. If you are not at peace with yourself, take a moment to ask yourself, "Why is there a war going on inside me? Who are the sides and with what am I actually at war?" Look for a third option or truce. Can you establish a treaty that may lead to peace eventually?
- When facing challenging people or circumstances, take in deep breaths and slowly release them. Relax and continue to breathe mindfully.
- Stop trying to control things and people that cannot be controlled. Accept life on life's terms, even if you don't like it. We all have to experience disappointment and you are no different.

A Final Reflection

You were not created to be an unsure, depressed, frustrated human. When you are entrenched in these feelings, you are self-absorbed, unplugged from the bigger picture, and unable to have empathy for yourself and those around you. Your creator has blessed you with many gifts—you do not want to look back on your life and regret that you didn't use them fully to live well and help others. Trust in the positive mystery of life, in your creator, that everything will be okay; that you are loved, supported, and not alone. When you can relax into this belief, you will grow in love and be a stronger, happier member of this tribe called the human race.

Appendix A

Chart 1.1	**Your Feelings**			
During the past week...	**Rarely or none of the time** (<1 day)	**Some** (a little of the time) **(1-2 days)**	**At least half the time (3-4 days)**	**Just about all the time (5-7 days)**
1. I was bothered by things that usually don't bother me.	0	1	2	3
2. I did not feel like eating; my appetite was poor.	0	1	2	3
3. I could not shake off the blues, even with others' help.	0	1	2	3
4. I felt that I was just as good as other people.	3	2	1	3
5. I had trouble keeping my mind on what I was doing.	0	1	2	0
6. I felt depressed.	0	1	2	3
7. I felt that everything I did was an effort.	0	1	2	3
8. I felt hopeful about the future.	3	2	1	0
9. I thought my life had been a failure.	0	1	2	3
10. I felt fearful.	0	1	2	3
11. My sleep was restless.	0	1	2	3
12. I was happy.	3	2	1	0
13. I talked less than usual.	0	1	2	3
14. I felt lonely.	0	1	2	3
15. People were unfriendly.	0	1	2	3
16. I enjoyed life.	3	2	1	0
17. I had crying spells.	0	1	2	3
18. I felt sad.	0	1	2	3
19. I felt that people disliked me.	0	1	2	3
20. I could not "get going."	0	1	2	3

Scoring: Your score is the sum of all twenty circled numbers. You will be comparing your score from week one to week three to week five. A decreasing score shows that your depression is getting better.

You may copy this chart for your personal use only. To request permission to reproduce for other purposes, contact editor@sunriseriverpress.com

Chart 4.1	**Week** _____						
	Day 1 Date:	Day 2 Date:	Day 3 Date:	Day 4 Date:	Day 5 Date:	Day 6 Date:	Day 7 Date:
Time of day							
Type of exercise							
Intensity (easy-hard)							
How long?							
Pre-exercise mood							
Post-exercise mood							
Music, TV, other notes							

Chart 8.4 **Tracking Your Feelings**							
Feeling	**Mon**	**Tues**	**Wed**	**Thurs**	**Fri**	**Sat**	**Sun**
Vulnerable							
Sad							
Pressured							
Challenged							
Ambivalent							
Hurt							
Caring							
Angry							
Jealous							
Cynical							
Aggressive							
Peeved							
Cheery							
Pleased							
Content							
Irritated							
Out of control							
Contemptuous							
Hopeful							
Cross							
Motivated							
Upset							
Enraged							
Exuberant							
Rejected							
Depressed							
Offended							
Guilty							
Anxious							
Defeated							
Open							
Threatened							
Bitter							
Confused							
Hopeless							
Driven							

Appendix B

For People with Disabilities

More 54 million Americans, or nearly 20 percent of the population, have a disability or activity limitation. Many individuals with disabilities have additional barriers that they must address that go beyond the more general excuses of "not enough time" or "exercise is boring."

If you have a disability, I encourage you to learn more about how you can participate in an exercise regimen. I want to get the word out about how important it is to get regular exercise to maintain one's daily function and quality of life. A basic workout program will make a huge difference in your life on so many levels, physically and emotionally. It will also give you greater appreciation for your body and more self-confidence in your appearance.

Here are some motivational quotes that can certainly be related to physical activity and improved health. Find your favorite and write it on an index card that is strategically placed around your home.

Unless you try to do something beyond
what you have already mastered, you will never grow.
— Ralph Waldo Emerson

Perseverance is not a long race; it is many short races, one after another.
— Walter Elliott

"You don't have to change that much for it to make a great deal of difference.
A few simple disciplines can have a major impact on how your life works out
in the next 90 days, let alone in the next 12 months or next 3 years."
— Jim Rohn

"You've got to get up every morning with determination
if you're going to go to bed with satisfaction."
— George Horace Lorimer

Look at a day when you are supremely satisfied at the end.
It's not a day when you lounge around doing nothing,
it's when you've had everything to do and you've done it!
— Margaret Thatcher

Tips

Learn more about exercise and how you can be active. Past frustrations should not stop you from using a fitness center. Yes, there are barriers, but there are also solutions:

• Surround yourself with people who support your new active lifestyle.
• Remove things from your environment that tempt you to be less active or eat less healthy.
• Determine activities that you enjoy doing instead of watching television (or other sedentary behaviors).
• Reward yourself for a job well done.
• Continually recommit to your decision to be more active.
• Take note of how exercise makes you feel healthier and remind yourself of these things.

More and more, diverse groups of "real" people are using fitness centers, including older adults, people who are obese, and others who have never before exercised. These changing user groups are beginning to force fitness centers to offer a more welcoming environment for people with disabilities, but many owners and operators of fitness centers are still not aware of the barriers that make using their facilities difficult for people with activity limitations or disabilities.

Like other public places, fitness centers must provide equal access to their facility for people with disabilities.

The following are resources to help you work within your disability to get to the activities you believe you will enjoy:

Checklist for Readily Achievable Barrier Removal – an easy-to-use survey tool to help people identify barriers in their facilities: http://www.usdoj.gov/crt/ada/checkweb.htm.

U.S. Access Board – an independent federal agency that provides exten-
sive information on ADA Accessibility Guidelines: http://www.
access-board.gov or (800) 872-2253.
ADA Accessibility Guidelines for Recreation Facilities: http://www.
access-board.gov/recreation/final.htm.
ADA & IT Technical Assistance Centers – regional resource centers that
provide information on the ADA: http://www.dbtac.vcu.edu/ or
(800) 949-4232.

Fitness Center Accessibility Resources

Access Equals Opportunity: Recreation Facilities & Fitness Centers:
http://www.metrokc.gov/dias/ocre/fun.htm.
National Center on Physical Activity and Disability – a resource center
that offers information on increasing access to exercise and fitness
centers: http://www.ncpad.org or (800)900-8086.
AIMFREE (Accessibility Instruments Measuring Fitness and Recreation
Environments)- checklists to help identify barriers in fitness centers. http://www.ncpad.org/yourwrites/fact_sheet.php?sheet=481or
(800)900-8086 (voice and TTY).
Choosing a Fitness Center, 2006: http://www.ncpad.org/exercise/fact_
sheet.php?sheet=359&view=all .
Rehabilitation Engineering Research Center on Recreation Technologies
(RERC Rec-Tech) – dedicated to using technology to promote more
healthy, active lifestyles for people with disabilities and offers a list of
accessible fitness equipment: http://www.rectech.org/ or (312) 413-
1955 (voice and TTY).
Removing Barriers to Health Clubs and Fitness Facilities – a guide to
making fitness centers more accessible for people with disabilities:
http://www.fpg.unc.edu/~ncodh/pdfs/rbfitness.pdf.

Index

Acknowledgments

Many thanks are owed to my family and friends who have supported me and given me assistance in preparing this book. My experience with the team at Sunrise River Press has been nothing short of extraordinary. Their faith in me as a new author and the ease in which we collaborated on this project have been true gifts. Throughout this book, I present vignettes as a means of illustrating how people can change and get better. Know that I have changed these stories and altered the identities of those described, focusing solely on the process of healing and how that may be beneficial to you, the reader. I am so fortunate to have worked with such amazing men and women who have walked through my office door. I am quite sure I've gotten as much or more from the relationships as I hope they have found with me. It is, therefore, my pleasure to play it forward.

About the Author

Jane Baxter, PhD, is a psychotherapist and certified physical trainer who has developed an innovative approach to improving patients' physical and mental health simultaneously. Dr. Baxter received her PhD and MSW in Clinical Social Work from the University of Maryland. A specialist in mood disorders and binge eating and other addictions, Dr. Baxter has proven that patients can train their brains the same way they train and strengthen their bodies. Her psychotherapy sessions unite physical workouts and instruction with tradi-  tional talk therapy in a unique treatment process she calls PsychFit. Dr. Baxter is based in Washington, D.C.

Also Available from Sunrise River Press

Answers to Anorexia

A Breakthrough Nutritional Treatment That Is Saving Lives

James M. Greenblatt, MD This new medical treatment plan for anorexia nervosa is based on cutting-edge research on nutritional deficiencies and the use of a simple but revolutionary brain test that can help psychiatrists select the best medication for an individual. Anorexia is a complex disorder with genetic, biological, psychological, and cultural contributing factors; it is not primarily a psychiatric illness as has been believed for so long. Dr. Greenblatt has helped many patients with anorexia recover simply by correcting specific nutritional deficiencies, and here he explains which nutrients must be supplemented as part of treatment. He finally offers patients and their families new hope for successful treatment of this serious, frustrating, and enigmatic illness. Softbound, 6 x 9 inches, 288 pages. Item # SRP607

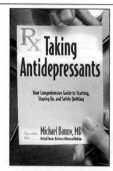

Taking Antidepressants

Your Comprehensive Guide to Starting, Staying On, and Safely Quitting

by Michael Banov, MD Antidepressants are the most commonly prescribed class of medications in this country. Yet, consumers have few available resources to educate them about starting and stopping antidepressants. Dr. Michael Banov walks the reader through a personalized process to help them make the right choice about starting antidepressants, staying on antidepressants, and stopping antidepressants. Readers will learn how antidepressant medications work, what they may experience while taking them, and will learn how to manage side effects or any residual or returning depression symptoms. Softbound, 6 x 9 inches, 304 pages. Item # SRP606

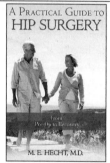

A Practical Guide to Hip Surgery

From Pre-Op to Recovery

M.E. Hecht, MD This book tells you everything you need to know before you undergo hip replacement or resurfacing surgery, directly from an orthopedic surgeon who has performed countless hip surgeries and has undergone a double hip replacement herself! Dr. M.E. Hecht tells you step by step what you'll need to do to before the day of your surgery, and then walks you through the procedure itself so that you know exactly what to expect. Sharing from her own experience as a hip surgery patient, she also discusses issues that can arise during the first few days through first months of your recovery, and includes handy checklists to help you organize and plan for your post-surgery weeks so you can focus on recovering as quickly and smoothly as possible. This book is a must-read before you undergo surgery, and will prove to be a trusted and essential resource during and after your hospital stay. Softbound, 6 x 9 inches, 160 pages. Item # SRP612

Manage Your Depression through Exercise

The Motivation You Need to Start and Maintain an Exercise Program

Jane Baxter, PhD Research has proven that exercise helps to lessen or even reverse symptoms of depression. Most depressed readers already know they need to exercise, but many can't muster the energy or motivation to take action. *Manage Your Depression through Exercise* is the only book on the market that meets depressed readers where they are at emotionally, physically, and spiritually and takes them from the difficult first step of getting started toward a brighter future. Through the Move & Smile Five-Week Activity Plan, the Challenge & Correct Formula to end negative self-talk, and words of encouragement, author Jane Baxter uses facts, inspiration, compassion, and honesty to help readers get beyond feelings of inertia one step at a time. Includes reproducible charts, activities list, positive inner-dialogue comebacks, and photos illustrating various exercises. Softbound, 6 x 9 inches, 192 pages. Item # SRP624